he's having a baby

he's having a baby

Jack O'Sullivan
and David Thomas

A Dorling Kindersley Book

LONDON, NEW YORK, MELBOURNE,
MUNICH, AND DELHI

Senior Editor Paula Regan
Designer Katie Eke
DTP Design Adam Walker
Production Controller Melanie Dowland
Picture Research Sarah Hopper

Managing Editor Julie Oughton
Managing Art Editor Heather McCarry
Art Director Peter Luff
Publisher – Special Projects Stephanie Jackson
Publisher Corinne Roberts

First published in Great Britain in 2005 by
Dorling Kindersley Limited
80 Strand
London WC2R 0RL

A Penguin Company

2 4 6 8 10 9 7 5 3 1

A CIP catalogue record for this book is
available from the British Library.

ISBN 1 4053 1261 0

Printed and bound by MOHN Media,
Mohndruck GmbH, Germany

Discover more at
www.dk.com

Contents

Foreword

I love having babies. No I mean it, I actually love giving birth, the whole experience from beginning to end. Having a baby for me is orgasmic, better than any drug you can take. When my babies popped out I wanted to stand naked on the highest mountain and roar with pride. I wanted to do it again and again and again.

But you chaps don't get to experience the joys of childbirth, in fact men largely get ignored when it comes to the whole pregnancy, birth, and becoming a parent thing. But fear not, help is at hand.

BBC's *He's Having A Baby* takes a cross section of British men and follows their unique stories all the way to the birth of their children and beyond. It really gets to the heart of what it takes to be a 21st-century super dad. Nothing like this has ever been attempted before – it really is the mother (and father) of all TV shows. And this book, to accompany the series, is your very own DIY guide to fatherhood.

Fear not, help is at hand

Exactly how do dads become dads? What exactly is father material? (Can you buy it on eBay?) Do all men have a hidden "hero switch" that is flicked from Off to On the moment their child is born?

This book will answer these questions and loads more and hopefully make you the kind of father who wants to do it all again and again and again…

Davina
xx

Davina McCall

Introduction

This book is about probably the most important thing you will ever do. Your child, the small person whose arrival makes you open this page, is your legacy. At the end of your life, what will really have mattered? Your job? Yes, a bit. Your football team? Mmmm – perhaps more. But weighing it all up, many of us will return to memories of that warm, fretful body dangling on our shoulder in the middle of night, as we struggled to hum another tune. "Did I do a good job?" we will ask, thinking of the person that baby grew into.

You know much more than you think

Being a dad can be tough, but you start with a great advantage. You are a hero and everyone loves a good dad, especially your child. Perhaps you don't feel all that heroic now. You're not alone. Many of us, for example, don't intend to become dads, at least not when it happens. Maybe you think you aren't ready (no one ever is). You will learn – more than you thought possible. Perhaps you feel confused and ignorant, anxious about money. It's hardly surprising. We storm into fatherhood with little preparation. And the juggling act isn't easy. We want to earn for our families, but have time to enjoy our children. Getting the balance right seems impossible when the ground rules are so unclear.

There is no right way to be a dad, so, if you feel uncomfortable, you aren't necessarily breaking a rule. You have to choose your own way. That means believing in yourself and your instincts. If that sounds like a blind man wandering off alone into the desert, have more faith. In the coming pages, you'll find hard evidence showing just how good dads' instincts are. We know much more than we think.

You can be just as sensitive to a baby's cries as a woman. Within hours of the birth, dads can recognize their babies blindfolded, by the touch and shape of their hands. If you feel ham-fisted, remember that new mums make just as many mistakes starting out.

However, you face an important question. You are a dad in a culture that makes few concessions to fatherhood. So you have to make a decision to be your own man, to be part of a generation shaping a new fatherhood. You won't regret it.

Jack O'Sullivan

JACK O'SULLIVAN

Jack is a co-founder of Fathers Direct, the UK National Information Centre on Fatherhood, where the team has developed much of the thinking for this book. A former Associate Editor of *The Independent*, he is also founding editor of *Dad*, the men's magazine for new fathers. Jack has written for many years on health and social policy and is a former Harkness Fellow of the Commonwealth Fund of New York. He lives in Oxfordshire with Hester, his wife, and their two children, Sophie (age 8) and Freddie (age 3).

DAVID THOMAS

David, author of the "The Teenage Years" chapter, is a former editor of *Punch* magazine and a regular contributor to the *Daily Mail* and *Sunday Telegraph*. He has written extensively on men's issues and fatherhood, and is author of *Not Guilty: In Defence of the Modern Man*, and *Foul Play*, an investigation into football match-fixing that was short-listed for the William Hill Sports Book of the Year. He lives in Sussex with Clare, his wife, and their three children, Holly (age 17), Lucy (age 16), and Fred (age 7).

Why **dads matter**

You will always matter hugely to her, even if she has never met you. Be more than a dream, hold her hand, and she'll do better at school, in life. Cherish her hugs and kisses and, when she's older, she'll love herself and find lasting love more easily. Ignore the voices that write you off. When in doubt, listen to your child.

Ten reasons why you matter

Some people think your job only really starts when your son can kick a ball or your daughter needs a taxi driver. But 700 research papers published annually prove beyond doubt that paternity is indispensable.

1 Who else, other than mum, will tuck her into bed at night, teach her how to ride a bike, fund her first holiday with friends, and buy her first pint?

2 He's got your genes. You are part of his history, who he is, how he looks, right down to those big ears and awkward gait.

3 You matter to your partner, too. When you get stuck in from the start, breastfeeding is more successful and she is less likely to suffer postnatal depression.

4 You'll raise brainy kids. Children with involved fathers have better social skills when they reach nursery and do better in examinations at 16.

5 Being a good dad keeps your child sane. Father-child closeness is a crucial predictor of long-term mental health.

6 Successful professional women tend to have at least one thing in common: fathers who respect and encourage them.

7 Do well as a father and, when your child's time comes, she'll be a better mum.

8 You'll keep him out of the clink. Good fathering means your son is less likely to have a criminal record.

9 She'll be happier later: father involvement at age 7 is correlated with your daughter's contentment with love at 33.

10 Do you want your child to have higher self-esteem, be friendly, and trust others? Your influence makes a difference.

CHILD TALK

"There you were when I was born, holding me in your arms."
Mairead (age 11)

"Some people say 'like father like son'. But I think they are wrong. Like father like daughter. I'm exactly like my dad. Not in looks. In personality. We both like fishing and picnics."
Emma (age 11)

"My dad loves and cares for me, yet he still has time to watch the football."
Tom (age 8)

"I don't like it when my dad's at work because I really miss him. He doesn't need to give me much because I know he loves me."
Jenny (age 9)

"I would like my dad to take me out to fun places and see him every day. I wish I could go to him when I need to solve my problems. I want him to live in my house, next door to my room."
Daniel (age 11)

"My daddy takes me to see the ducks."
Shaun (age 4)

Daddy **cool**

Worried that fatherhood means the death of cool? Have no fears. With a new child, you enter a club that stars are jostling to join. The emotion seems to have got to a few of them, producing lines worthy of the craziest Hollywood scriptwriter.

"Some people have got advice, some people have got horror stories. I like people that look you in the eye with a glow and say, 'It's gonna be cool.'"
Russell Crowe anticipates the birth

"I've made a few nice dishes in my time, but this must be the best I've ever made."
Jamie Oliver on Daisy, his second child

I spoke to Luca on the phone and he burped. I was in tears. He looks like a turnip, but a beautiful turnip."
Colin Firth, star of Bridget Jones's Diary, gets sentimental

"All my boys have girlfriends and I keep telling them to be careful. I don't want to be a grandad yet."
Mel Gibson on having five teenage sons

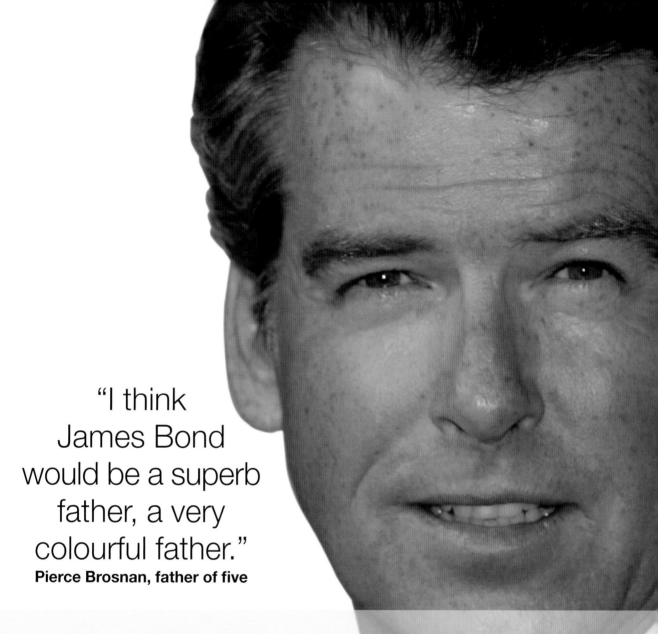

"I think James Bond would be a superb father, a very colourful father."
Pierce Brosnan, father of five

"I am neither. My favourite role is father."
**Lenny Kravitz after being asked
whether he prefers to be a rock god or a sex god**

"After all my success, I feel incredibly free and can now be a better father and husband. Being a father is fantastic."
Michael Douglas aims high

You and **your dad**

Our own dads often seem light years away as we contemplate fatherhood. He may have been written off as the walking wallet, a man who could change a light bulb but certainly not a nappy. Yet, sometimes, when I cuddle our son to sleep or play with our daughter, I think: "This feels very familiar; he did this with me" and a light begins to fall on a hidden history.

Understanding your upbringing is the first step towards giving your own children the best start in life

Most of us don't talk to our own dads about what lies ahead, perhaps because of the great cultural change going on. In Sweden, where the "New Dad" has been around for 30 years, 70 per cent of dads say their own fathers' experience offers at least some positive guidance on how to do the job today. Elsewhere in the world this figure is much lower, and most men say their father has no influence at all. We're making it up as we go along.

Your own brand

But it's actually not a great idea to think of this as Year Zero, when you forget the past, mixing up a bit of David Beckham with some Arnold Schwarzenegger and a smattering of Homer Simpson to create your own unique brand of modern paternity. Because understanding your upbringing is a first, vital step towards giving your own children the best start in life.

Examining the past

Psychologists have been researching dads in mass studies for about 35 years and they have made a stunning finding. "Expectant" dads who have successfully examined their own childhoods and understand their relationships with their own parents go on to produce happier and better emotionally adjusted children. You don't need a happy childhood to be a good dad. But it helps to understand how it affected you.

Your dad as grandad

It's also worth remembering that, as you become a dad, your father, if he is still alive, is becoming a grandfather. The birth of your son or daughter is a huge opportunity for him as well, a chance, because he probably has fewer work responsibilities, to do things differently. He may need help and encouragement. You *can* teach the old dog new tricks.

WHAT'S THE BEST AGE TO BE A DAD?

Age 30 is the average, but one in five new dads is under 18 or over 40, with one in a hundred over 50.

There is no perfect age, despite excitement about film stars becoming dads in their sixties and the bad press that teenage dads get. In fact, young dads are very active, often more used to children, though less likely to last the course. Older dads tend to be fathers by choice, positive about the prospect, and happy to take a lot of responsibility for young children. They behave more like mothers, smiling and chatting with a baby, but aren't so good at getting down on the floor. But like very young dads, they may be strapped for cash, due to second families or having passed their peak earning years. There are pluses and minuses at every age – the trick is to make the best of yourself.

Quick quiz
what type of dad will you be?

Will you be Super Dad, Fun Dad, or Slack Dad? The choice is yours. Try our paternity test and find out where you're heading.

1 **Ideally, you want your baby to be:**

a Held lovingly by you in constant skin-to-skin contact, because every moment is a wonderful, bonding opportunity.

b In a cot close by in case she needs you at night.

c As far away as possible.

2 **Your volatile boss insists you attend his office party while your partner is in labour. You say:**

a "Keep up that talk and it'll be your funeral."

b "Sorry I can't make it, but we wonder if you would like to be a godfather?"

c "Great. The missus and the baby should be along later if they get a move on."

3 **Your partner asks whether you prefer Huggies. Do you:**

a Consult your copy of *What Nappy Weekly*?

b Tell her that you will change nappies but she can choose them?

c Think this is a come-on line and start humming "Tonight's the night"?

4 **As a dad, you want to be like:**

a Mufasa, the Lion King.

b Homer Simpson.

c Captain Hook.

5 **Your baby wakes up for the tenth time in the night. Do you:**

a Merrily jump out of bed singing "Let's Rock Around the Clock Tonight"?

b Sleep until your partner finishes breastfeeding, then wind the baby?

c Hide under the duvet, showing all the enthusiasm of an ageing sloth?

6 **You think the typical child is:**

a Macaulay Culkin in *Home Alone*.

b Ron Weasley in *Harry Potter*.

c Damien in *The Omen*.

7 Your baby pukes on your best suit? You say:

a "My darling baby, no fragrance is as lovely as yours. Wait till I show this to everyone in the office."

b "I've always hated pinstripes."

c "I've always hated babies."

8 You hear that babies cost a fortune. Your reaction is:

a "I don't care, even if it means trading in the Porsche for a lawn mower."

b "Time we got the grandparents to chip in a bit financially."

c "Really! How much can we sell this one for?"

ANSWERS

If you picked:

Mostly **a** You're Super Dad and a loving partner, perhaps too perfect and indeed a touch scary.

Mostly **b** You're a realistic Fun Dad, prone to mistakes but your heart's in the right place.

Mostly **c** You are Slack Dad, woefully unprepared for fatherhood. It's time to shape up – fast!

great
expectations

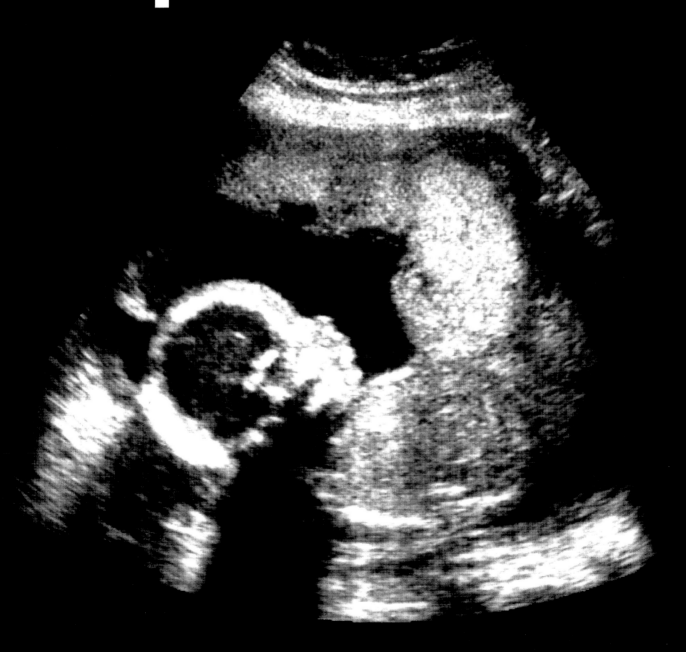

"Yeeees"…"Oh no! Please God, don't let this be true"…**"Shouldn't I be feeling something?"**…"How will we manage?"…"But you said it was safe"…"I need a new job"…**"Is it a boy or a girl?"**…"Sit down, I'll make you a cup of tea"…**"I'm taking a walk"**.

Hearing that a baby is on the way invokes terror, delight, sometimes total numbness. **Nothing will ever be the same again**. Many of us storm into fatherhood, ignorant and **emotionally unprepared**, with little but instinct as a mentor. Yet, in each man sits a deep well from which to draw **the makings of a great dad**.

She's **pregnant!**

When did we make love? Is she late or was that just a light one? Is she pregnant or isn't she? She disappears with a testing kit and emerges in tears. There is elation, the shock of conception, the first feelings of anxiety for a child that will carry on for life. And vomiting. Some women escape completely but for a few "morning sickness" respects no hour of pregnancy. A wise man doesn't remind her that it's a good sign.

WHAT HAPPENS WHEN

It's going to be a bumpy few months. Here's what to expect:

1–13 weeks

- Conception: your sperm fuses with her egg, the cells divide and travel down the Fallopian tube until, perhaps a week after fertilization, implantation in the womb.

- By 8 weeks you should know whether she is pregnant. Your baby is about the size of a strawberry.

- At 12 weeks the baby is fully-formed including tiny fingers, toes, and ears. A face is recognizable, nostrils have formed, and there is already a tongue. The foetus is about 6.5cm (2½in) long and weighs about 18g (5/8oz). You can see the first antenatal scan, which should show any abnormalities.

- Up to 25 per cent of pregnancies end in miscarriage in this time, often without either of you knowing.

- She will feel very tired.

14–27 weeks

- After 14 weeks, morning sickness is over for most women, who normally start to feel a lot better.

- At 16 weeks, your baby is about 16cm (6in) long and weighs about 135g (4¾oz). His neck is visible and he already has his own unique fingerprint pattern. He can suck his thumb and has fine, downy hairs on his face and body (called lanugo). His heart

So what are you thinking?

It's a phantom pregnancy? Perhaps you are ready, few men are. But, there is time to let it all sink in. No need to rush to tell friends before 12 weeks. Miscarriage is very common and rarely discussed, so don't count your chickens yet. However, with the ultrasound scan, the physical reality begins to dawn. The heartbeat pounds – astonishingly strong – and you will feel a lump in your throat. There is a living creature, partly you, inside her. It is just a few centimetres long.

There may be more scans, fears of defects as your baby grows more real, and some hard decisions.

Denial time is over

Once all the tests are done, inevitability calls for acceptance. You *will* be a dad. There is nesting to be done, DIY. The bump gets bigger and kicks. You become your mate's domestic slave. Discomfort finally robs her – and you – of sleep. But nothing, not even the antenatal classes and midwife visits, prepares you for what comes next.

There is a living creature, partly you, inside her…you *will* be a dad

beats at twice his mother's rate. Your partner's "bump" will start to show.

- At 20 weeks you can learn the sex of the baby from a scan. Your baby starts moving.

- Particularly after 20 weeks, watch out for pre-eclampsia. The causes of pre-eclampsia are unknown, but symptoms include high blood pressure, sudden weight gain, changes in vision, swollen limbs and face. If the condition goes untreated and progresses into eclampsia, the mother can suffer thrombosis, brain haemorrhage, and coma, threatening the lives of both mother and baby. Very young and older mothers are most at risk.

- 24 weeks is the latest date for a termination.

- At 26 weeks, he is potentially viable outside the womb.

28–40 weeks

- At 25 weeks you must warn your boss about your paternity leave.

- By 36 weeks early delivery is no longer a problem.

- 40 weeks is full term.

- At 42 weeks some babies, especially first ones, are late, but most hospitals induce once a baby is 14 days overdue.

Getting involved
while she's getting bigger

You may think, once you've proved your fertility, that's your
job done for nine months. No chance. He can hear your
low-pitched voice more clearly than hers before he is born.
And he'll certainly recognize hers, asking you to rub her
feet. So don't hold back: get stuck in right from the start.

Hard labour for you, too...

1 Be ready with the sick bowl.

2 Bite your tongue when she gets ratty. It's good preparation for the obscenities she'll roar at the birth.

3 Keep talking to her about how you feel, about what you both may be losing and gaining.

4 Find a (male) friend to talk to. Your partner might not have space to hear some of the things you need to say.

5 Shop, cook, clean, decorate. When exhausted, try not to say "Who's having this baby, you or me?".

6 Go with your partner to antenatal appointments, so you can hear the baby's heartbeat and watch him move on the monitor.

7 If anyone tries to exclude you, remind them tactfully that when dad is well-informed, mothers typically have shorter labours and need less pain relief.

8 Don't be afraid to see a doctor or midwife alone. You can ask questions that might worry your partner.

9 Go to antenatal classes. Never mind if they hum, sit cross-legged, and burn candles. You'll learn a lot.

10 Remind her of how great she looks as she gets bigger.

SEX AND PREGNANCY

Strange as it seems, it's probably best to use a condom, to protect against infection and a male hormone that can induce labour. But penetrative sex is not normally a risk to the baby. The author, Karen Krizanovich, who writes on relationships, comments: "Some women are as horny as hell through the entire pregnancy, but mostly they feel fat, tired, grumpy, and totally unattractive." Junior doesn't help if he joins in on the act and kicks you in the stomach. The key to happy sex is giving her lots of loving, caring, cuddling, and intimacy. She'll feel better, and who knows where that might lead.

WHAT HAPPENS AT AN ANTENATAL CLASS?

"Imagine you have a pencil up your backside and you're writing your name with it," says the antenatal instructor. Sixteen adults duly crouch on all fours, looking like cows with a writing problem. "Full name or just the first?" I gasp, as she leads us through the physical difficulties of having a baby. It's a good laugh, a chance to learn about childbirth, to take a couple of hours a week to focus on the baby together, and make some good friends. Don't miss it.

Their **health** and yours

Your partner may have a lot to cope with during pregnancy, such as morning sickness, fatigue, mood swings, heartburn, constipation, haemorrhoids (piles), varicose veins – and that's the easy stuff. More serious can be fear of miscarriage, diabetes, and pre-eclampsia (*see p.21*), linked to high blood pressure.

If you want to be around for your children when they are older, take care of yourself now

So she needs looking after. Offer her frequent snacks, such as bananas or crackers, to keep her health up during morning sickness. Encourage her to rest, especially in the tiring first 12 weeks of pregnancy. Then keep her off ladders, when she gets a burst of energy later on.

Good food is vital

Support your partner by sharing her diet. Carbohydrates such as pasta, pulses, and potatoes will keep her energy up. Fish, poultry, pasteurized dairy products, cereals, seeds, and pulses provide the protein for your baby's growth. Fresh fruit and vegetables provide the vitamin C she needs daily. She'll also need iron from red meat and fish to avoid anaemia. The combination of all these foods ensures a good dose of vitamin B complex.

Gentle exercise

Taking up marathon running or mountain climbing with her is not a good idea. But you could both do some gentle exercise together. Swimming is great so she can feel weightless in the water. Walking is good, especially in later pregnancy, for positioning the baby ready for birth. Encourage your partner to exercise her pelvic floor muscles – which can weaken during pregnancy – to help support her bowel, bladder, and womb.

Keeping your baby well

Stop smoking and encourage your partner to quit too: a foetus's growth can be stunted by anyone smoking nearby. Alcohol can damage a baby's development. She will find it easier to stop drinking if you do, too. Always wash fruit, vegetables, and your hands: under-cooked meat and animal faeces used in fertilizers can contain toxoplasma, a chemical of serious danger to unborn babies.

CUT THE CAFFEINE

Expectant dads should be wary of encouraging their pregnant partners to sit down and enjoy a cup of coffee. Drinking more than eight cups of coffee a day during pregnancy doubles the risk of having a still-born baby.

HELPING HAND

You'll do better if you know more, so check out:
- **Fathers Direct**
Lots of information for every kind of dad.
www.fathersdirect.com
- **Families Need Fathers**
Experts on issues about separation.
08707 607496 (evenings only: 7pm–10pm)
www.fnf.org.uk
- **Parentline Plus**
24-hour freephone service for parents.
0808 800 2222
www.parentlineplus.org.uk
- **Sure Start**
Information about local services for parents.
0800 096 0296
www.surestart.gov.uk

FIT FOR THE JOB

You may feel that the last person you should be thinking of is yourself, but you're wrong. Here's five reasons why:

1 Keep fit with a balanced diet and you will have more energy, more patience, and a more positive state of mind than if you slob out.

2 Children are more likely to take exercise if dad does, so start now to set a good example later.

3 If you want to be around for your children when they are older, take care of yourself now to help ensure a healthy future.

4 Those who exercise regularly for ten years are five times less likely to die from a heart attack at 59.

5 A good diet and giving up smoking may save you from cancer — the second biggest dad killer.

Sort out **your money**

It's called "provider fever" when a man breaks into a cold sweat at the very thought of how much it costs to be a father. It can last longer than morning sickness but a quick cure is to fix your finances upfront.

How much will it *really* cost?

It is important to know that having children does not cost the fortune that the newpapers claim. The reality is that your whole life changes and you just spend your money differently. The key is to budget – calculate how much money you have, reassess how it is spent, and decide exactly where it should go. You will feel happier and more in control.

Life insurance

Protect yourself and your family. You will need life insurance worth 10–20 times your current salary, so that, if you died, your family would not be any poorer. A cheaper solution is a policy that, if you died, would pay an annual sum until your children are, say, 21 but which lapses if you survive beyond that time. Don't forget to insure your partner. If she died, you would need the money for child care, even if you carried on working.

Financial help

There is some help available from the Government. Child Benefit is paid monthly to either you or your baby's mother and there is Child Tax Credit for taxpayers. Every new baby is entitled to a minimum of £250 from the Government paid into a Child Tax Fund. Be sure to register for these benefits. Even the smallest sum saved regularly can make a big difference for the future. If you are not living with your child, make a private agreement with your baby's mother about how much to pay, or contact the Child Support Agency. Then pay weekly by cheque or standing order – but not in cash, as proof of payment can be important.

AGONY UNCLE

Q: I see what my neighbours spend on their kids. I just don't know how I'll ever manage to be a good dad.

A: "Kids don't have to drain your wallet", according to Wayne Hemingway, fashion designer, style guru, and father of four. "Do kids need to wear logos? No! Why pay to be a walking billboard. Do kids constantly need taking to bowling alleys, multiplexes, and fast-food outlets? Do they need new toys every few weeks? No, no, no! They need your time, a game in the park, a cycle, good old-fashioned hide-and-seek. As long as you're putting your heart into it, it beats Playstation every time. If your kids only react to money spent on them, you're failing them as a dad. That's far worse than failure in anything else."

WAYS TO CUT COSTS

1 Spend an hour a month planning a budget. Work out your income and likely outgoings: food, clothes, transport, rent or mortgage, gas, electricity, television, and so on.

2 Borrow baby clothes and accessories or buy second hand.

3 Rather than buying new, use your local library for books and DVDs.

4 Shop around: you could make big annual savings if you switch your supermarket, change your gas and electricity suppliers, and rotate your credit.

5 In times of dire straits, raid your child's piggy bank – but pay it back with interest.

Getting ready:
planning the birth together

You were there at the start of all this. So make sure you support your partner in preparing for the next bit; in helping choose how your baby is born and what happens next.

HEALTHY HOME

- Slap bright colours on the walls of your baby's room. Infants are short-sighted and need stimuli.
- Buy a couple of simple toys the baby can suck.
- Get a plastic baby rest for the bath – it's safer.
- Keep pets out of the way: they can spread germs.
- Clear floors of small things a baby might swallow.
- Install plug-socket guards.
- Place a fireguard around the hearth and cover sharp edges with tape.
- Cover glass doors with anti-shatter plastic film.
- Create a safe area in which to leave your baby (such as a playpen downstairs).
- Ensure you have a comfortable chair to sit in with your baby.

Birth plan

Most couples write a birth plan with the midwife so everyone can remember in the heat of the moment how you both wanted things to be. It's all very flexible, and your partner might change her mind on the day. But writing everything down helps you think ahead and will give you confidence at the birth. A plan tackles whether your partner wants a home or hospital birth. It can specify how long you, the father, would like to stay in the hospital after the birth, how much of a Caesarean you might want to see, and whether you want to cut the umbilical cord. These days, some dads actually help with the delivery.

Know your "BRAN"

As you and your partner consider the choices about medical interventions, such as home versus hospital birth, keep "BRAN" at the back of your mind. Ask what are the benefits (B), the risks to your partner (R), the alternatives (A), and what would happen if she chose to have no medical intervention (N).

Hospital visit

It's a good idea to visit the hospital with your partner beforehand. You'll get a sense of how warm and caring the atmosphere is – and it's also a chance to check out the route so you don't get lost on the big day. Ask what pain relief is available (see p.39). Does the hospital have birthing pools? Are there beanbags and birthing stools provided so she will be comfortable? Can your partner move around during labour and give birth in the position she chooses? What happens if the labour gets difficult? Will you be allowed to stay with her at all times? Talk to other couples who have given birth there and ask about their experiences.

Overnight stay

Some maternity units have overnight facilities for dads. Ask about them or consider booking a private room for

Thinking ahead will give you confidence on the big day

after the birth. If you are lucky, some hospitals will let you sleep there, with mother and baby, in a chair or a fold-down bed. Staying overnight requires gentle diplomacy, pre-planning, and determination, but can be great for your partner and for being really involved right from the start.

You are important

More than nine out of ten fathers attend the delivery of their babies. Research shows that if you are with your partner, she is less likely to be distressed, will experience less pain, receive less medication, and feel more positive about the whole experience.

PATERNITY LEAVE: THE FACTS

You are entitled to two weeks paid paternity leave:

- The rate is low but many employers top it up.
- You don't have to be married to, or live with, the mother to be eligible.
- You can take your leave in one block or two separate weeks.
- You must warn your boss at least 15 weeks before your child is due and have worked there for at least 41 weeks before the due date.
- You can't take paternity leave before the birth, but you can take it earlier than planned if the birth is premature.
- Both you and your partner can also claim up to four weeks unpaid parental leave in the first year, and up to 13 weeks in the first five years.

MATERNITY LEAVE

New mothers are entitled to a year's maternity leave. The first six weeks are paid at 90 per cent of her salary, the next 20 at the same rate as for paternity leave, and the final 26 weeks are unpaid. Detailed rules apply, so she will need to check before the birth.

Don't forget the toothbrush

By now it's about 280 days since conception and here's your next big test: do you know the way to the hospital? Have you packed the right things in the bag? You don't actually need much – opposite are some recommended essentials. And maybe a map too?

THE ESSENTIALS

- Oil for massaging her

- Snacks to keep you both going, juice and water

- A water spray to keep her cool – a water pistol is less effective, but can lighten the atmosphere

- Swimming trunks to avoid shocking the midwife when you get into the pool or bath with your partner

- *War and Peace* (or any good book – labour can take a while)

- Her favourite CDs plus a portable player

- Nighties, knickers, and pads

- Mobile phone, or change for a payphone, plus a list of key numbers

- Pillows – hospitals never supply enough

- Camera and spare film

- Nappies

- Baby blanket

- A couple of baby gros

- Toothbrush and toothpaste

- Cigars

BE PREPARED

- Practise the route to the hospital at different times of the day so you really know how long it takes.

- Keep a mobile phone with you so you can be contacted easily.

- Have plenty of rest beforehand – you'll need it.

- Wear loose, cool clothes. Delivery rooms are very hot.

- Get your bag of essentials ready (*see left*).

- Eat well. You'll probably forget during labour.

She's **in labour!**

It can happen at any time, so be ready to drop everything. Be careful not to take on projects that absolutely require your presence. Make sure you are easily contactable and that people at work know you might leave in a hurry.

Five tell-tale signs

Your partner may experience pre-labour (or Braxton Hicks) contractions. They are variable, then stop abruptly. Her time is probably nigh, however, if she starts "nesting", rushing around tidying as though her mother-in-law is due any minute. This can carry on for days (or a lifetime!). Champagne, curry, even last-minute sex, are all said to speed things up.

1 Your partner might feel persistent lower-back pain and a need to urinate frequently as the baby positions itself for the birth.

2 She may have a "show" – when a pinkish "plug" of mucus that seals the womb comes away.

3 Her waters may break. If this is the only sign, however, don't rush into hospital: it may well be ages yet before she gives birth. Contact your midwife and ask for advice.

4 Real labour is indicated by slow, regular contractions getting steadily stronger, often with pain in the lower legs, the back and abdomen. If the waters haven't broken, there's no need to contact the midwife until contractions are ten minutes apart.

5 Established labour is marked by two to four contractions every ten minutes. If your partner isn't in the experts' hands by now, it's time to panic!

DAD TALK

"As their labour unfolds, I know that I am witnessing more than the birth of a baby. It is also the birth of a woman and a mother; the birth of a man and a father; the birth of a relationship that will never, ever be the same."
Lois Wilson, midwife

"The birth of a child goes way beyond words and opens up a world of emotion you never knew. Now, ravaged by sleepless nights, I cry all the time, my bowels smell evil (postnatal stress), and I can't lift my head off the pillow without help. It seems fatherhood has turned this particular man into a baby himself – but deep down, I know it is the other way around."
Andrew Purvis, father of three

HOW YOU CAN HELP HER

Caroline Flint, a midwife, explains: "When I was giving birth to my children, I couldn't have managed without my partner. I needed someone who cared for me more than anyone else – someone I could be horrible to when I was in pain but would still be there for me tomorrow. A man doesn't need to do much during labour. Just being there – having his smell and voice there – is virtually enough. Labour is like climbing Everest or running a marathon. It is difficult because it is so painful and you don't know when it will stop. Say things like: 'You're doing brilliantly darling, you brave woman'."

Real-life **birth stories**

Every father has his birth story – even if it's about missing the event. It describes perhaps the most profound moment of our lives. This common human event is, in each occurrence, utterly different and extraordinary. There are parallels in the animal world. Male seahorses, given the embryos by their partners, carry and nourish them for weeks before releasing them into the ocean. Male birds, rats, and primates instinctively dote on their newborn. A man's testosterone crashes by a third when a baby is born. Even watching videos of newborns sets off the reaction. So it's not surprising if you go soppy when your partner gives birth. It's your hormones. We're biologically programmed.

The easy birth

Nigel Evans recalls when his wife, Julie, gave birth to Tom:

"Julie woke up about 2 o'clock having big contractions. She went into the bathroom and said it had started. Unfortunately I was having a migraine and I was hoping that it was just a bad dream. She kept saying it had started and I was thinking: 'No, no, there's ages to go yet.' But she had had a couple of big contractions and then, about 20 minutes later, she had a huge one that almost didn't go away. She said: 'Nigel, I want to push.' I thought, 'Oh God, this is really happening.' So I rang an ambulance and midwife. I don't remember the migraine after that – the adrenalin must have cleared it.

"Fortunately, it never crossed my mind that I might have to deliver the baby, though Julie says that by then she had already decided that it could be up to me. The ambulance men arrived very quickly, took one look at her and said she wasn't going anywhere. This baby was coming now. They asked for warm towels – not hot water – and I stood by the bathroom door.

"Then the midwife arrived and Tom was born about five minutes

> A few pushes – no pain relief, nothing – and he was out

later. A few pushes – no pain relief, nothing – and he was out and fine. Julie and Tom were checked over and there was apparently no need for them to go to hospital. So the ambulance left and that was it. Suddenly, from it being just me and Julie, there was Tom as well. We just sat on the bed and looked at Tom. I felt really exhausted. Someone said: 'Another five minutes and you would have delivered him, Nigel', and the reality sank in. I felt a huge relief that everything was fine. I just thought 'Wow! Now I have a son.'"

> The reality sank in. I felt a huge relief that everything was fine

The difficult birth

Anthony McCarthy's wife, Phil, had twins, Áine and Jack: "It was a very anxious time. Phil was enormous and had been terribly sick during her pregnancy. We went to hospital because suddenly her blood pressure rocketed. We knew the danger of pre-eclampsia, that within a few minutes she could have an epileptic fit, fall into a coma, and could die. She had gone 40 weeks and was expecting twins, so she had 15 pounds of baby inside her.

"Phil was very worried about the babies and about her health. She knew that mothers should try to check the movements of the baby. But how do you check that *both* babies are moving?

"We arrived in the middle of a political war. The midwives believed everything should be natural, while the doctors were arguing that this was a very serious medical condition and they wanted Phil

> We knew, given the odds, that our two babies were vulnerable

heavily monitored. They were telling us that one in 80 babies was a twin but one in six babies in the neonatal intensive-care unit was a twin. So we knew, given these odds, that our two babies were vulnerable.

"The labour was long, exhausting, and very painful. We went into hospital and she started on Monday night about 8pm. She got me to tell her stories to distract her from the pain. Then at last, the following evening before midnight everything went very quiet. Phil really went into herself and was incredibly focused on getting these babies out. Áine was the first of the two to be born, at about 2am. It was wonderful – she was fine – and now

> Suddenly he opened his eyes and gave a little cry. We knew he was going to be alright

we could really concentrate on the other one. We knew the second twin was the vulnerable one. He was a long time coming – about 30 minutes in all. There were signs of distress: the monitor showed that his heart rate had risen. When Jack was born everyone could see he wasn't breathing. They said if he didn't breathe in the next 20 seconds he would be whisked off. I picked him up from the paediatrician and started imitating the gutteral sounds he was making in his throat. Suddenly, he opened his eyes and gave a little cry. It was a huge relief. We knew he was going to be alright."

The missed birth

Dean was not present at the birth of his son, Luke, but now looks after him full-time: "When I split up with my partner, she said that she was pregnant, but I didn't want to believe it. I was 19 and I didn't feel ready for the responsibility. When I didn't hear from her after that, I think I wanted to believe that she had been lying. But at the back of my mind I felt guilty. I was a bit in denial and it would have been so easy to carry on like that. But I had to make 100 per cent sure that she was lying. Each day, each month the pressure was building up.

"So I went to her house and found a baby who was three weeks old. I'd missed his birth. I had to believe what I saw. At first I wanted to make 100 per cent sure with a blood test, but that turned out to be difficult. I wanted to be sure because I knew if this really was my child, then I would do everything in my power to look after him. In the end, I just had faith that he was mine.

"I tried to support Luke and his mother, earning their keep. But she wasn't well and I could not stay there. About three months after he was born, there was a meeting of the social workers. They were talking about taking him into care. She couldn't cope. So I said I wasn't letting them take him into care. I would take him. There was nothing wrong with me. So he came to live with me. We went and lived with my mum at first and then we got our own place. It's been hard but we're OK. I'm sorry

> I went to her house and found a baby who was three weeks old. I'd missed his birth. I had to believe what I saw

I missed the birth, but maybe if I'm blessed, I can have another and get to see the birth then."

What's happening

...during the birth

I thought proving myself was about climbing a mountain, scoring a goal, getting a great job. Then, as I stood beside my partner through the delivery of our baby, I realized that it is about being there at the start and forever.

Q: I'm worried about the pain my partner will suffer. What can I do?

A: Keeping her upright and moving helps. Walk around with her, go to the hospital shop. Calm her. Pain can be tolerated much better in relaxed surroundings. Respect her decisions on pain relief and don't rush her into an epidural even if you find her pain distressing: epidurals can have negative side effects (*see opposite*).

Q: Labour can take ages. What else should I do?

A: A 12-hour labour or longer is not uncommon. Stay with your partner and encourage her. Don't panic. Give her sips of water, hold her hand, rub her back, and maintain eye contact. Remind her to go to the toilet. Don't read the paper.

Q: What will happen if the birth is not straightforward?

A: If the delivery is too slow, it can be assisted with forceps (which look like large metal salad servers) or ventouse (a suction cup that's fixed on to the baby's head). About one in five babies is born by Caesarean section. Half of Caesareans are planned during pregnancy and, in these cases, you can probably be present during the operation. If an emergency Caesarean has to be performed during labour, you may be asked to wait outside the operating theatre. Remember, even when the birth is tough and frightening, most fathers say, afterwards, that they wouldn't have missed it for the world.

Q: I can't stand the sight of blood. What if I faint?

A: There isn't usually much blood, at least until the final stage of labour when the placenta (afterbirth) comes away after the baby has been born. Old myths about fathers dropping like flies during labour are being disproved. One midwife who has delivered 1,200 babies has had only two dads keel over.

Q: Should I worry about the umbilical cord being caught around the baby's neck?

A: This sounds frightening, and can be dangerous. But it happens quite frequently, particularly just before the baby emerges. Your midwife will monitor the baby for any distress. It can be scary to see your baby emerge like this. But don't panic – midwives move quickly.

DAD TALK

"I held her hand and helped with the breathing. I was exhausted by the end of it and I didn't even have to do anything."
Kenny, clerical worker

PAIN RELIEF

TYPE	Pros	Cons
NATURAL: breathing, massage, and relaxation techniques, hot baths and water pools. The mother is kept active and able to move about.	Aims to produce shorter labour with the mother more likely to have a vaginal delivery.	Good in early labour, but may not be enough for the pain if the labour is long or the delivery has complications.
TENS MACHINES: wires attached to the back send tiny electrical currents to interrupt pain messages to the brain.	Woman can vary levels, stay in control, and stay mobile. This treatment does not affect the baby.	Can be irritating and ineffective for some women, particularly as the labour progresses.
ENTONOX: mixture of "laughing gas" (nitrous oxide) and oxygen, taken through a mask or mouthpiece, that can ease pain.	Easy to use, does not affect the baby, does not restrict movement, does not require monitoring of the mother, and can calm breathing.	Can cause nausea or make the mother feel "spaced out". Doesn't work for some mothers.
PETHIDINE: less popular now than in the past, this injection is related to morphine and helps relaxation.	Pain is less intense.	Crosses the placenta, so the baby may be "floppy" and need an antidote injection. The mother may vomit or feel nauseous, will need monitoring, and be less mobile.
EPIDURAL: anaesthetic injected via a plastic tube placed into the back near the spine.	Very effective in cutting pain. If an emergency Caesarean is needed, makes it quicker because the anaesthetic is already administered.	Requires a hospital birth and monitoring. Can slow labour and cause headaches and a rapid fall in blood pressure. Makes a Caesarean more likely.

What's happening

...immediately after

Hopefully, your baby will be fine. But there may have been complications. Checks will be made, the cord cut, and he'll be placed on your partner's body. He may be covered in blood and birth fluids, and look battered with pressure marks around his head. No need to panic – babies are tough.

Time out

The drama is over. Take some time. These are precious moments for you and your partner. You may feel like crying, you may feel stunned, you may not know quite how you feel. Talk to your baby. He knows your voice already. Tell your partner she is wonderful – she has been through so much. If the labour has been long and she has had a lot of pain relief, she may feel woozy. Be together. Don't just take the photos – be in them, too. From an early age, your children will delight in looking at them, hearing every detail of what mum and dad did just after they were born.

Breaking the news

Then, when you and your partner have had some peace, ring relatives and friends. It's a parent's privilege to break the news, so don't let others do it unless you want them to. Bring the phone to your partner if you can, so she can speak, too.

Visiting hours

Try, very diplomatically, to stay with your partner as long as you can. Sadly some hospitals can still be brutal, sending dads home soon after the birth, but, even if you have to leave, get back quickly.

Be there

She has been through a gruelling experience. She may be very sore after delivery by Caesarean section or because of an episiotomy (a small cut to widen the vaginal opening) and feel under pressure to begin breastfeeding as soon as possible. Given the shortage of midwives, your partner will really need you.

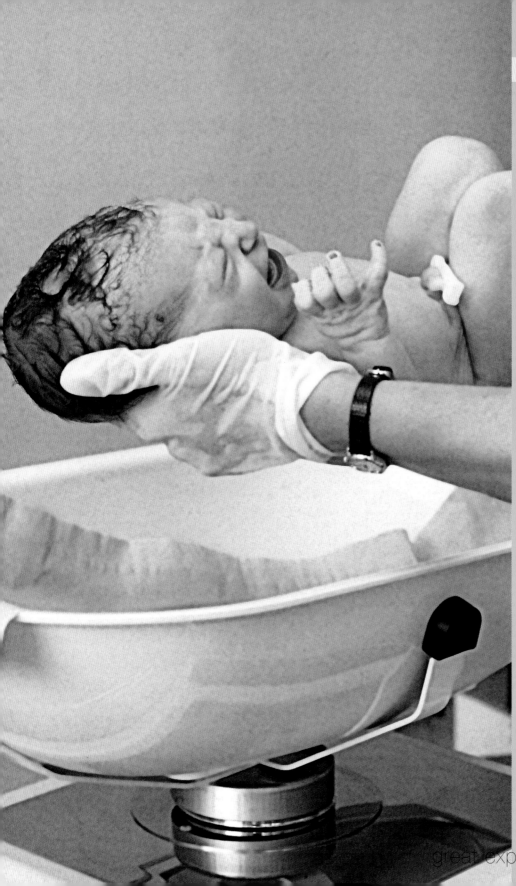

John and Linda Spencer had an extraordinary Valentine's Day. They awoke in a large, well-appointed room with a double bed and en-suite bathroom. They were not, however, in a smart hotel but in a maternity unit. Their son, Felix, had been born the previous evening and was asleep between them. To top it all, John was able to serve his wife breakfast in bed.

He was there to care for Linda and to look after Felix, changing nappies, washing, and dressing their newborn son. "It was so much better than after the births of our other children," recalls John, father of four. "When our daughter, Rosie, was born, I had to leave soon afterwards. I was drained, a bit bewildered, wondering what to do. I just ended up thinking about what to get the older children for tea.

"Having to leave like that can take the shine off having a new baby and unbalance you. You feel jealous that you are not there in hospital enjoying the first moments, too. You don't immediately want to be at home with another older child who wants to do colouring or be fed. You want to be with your wife and new baby."

Going **home**

PARENTAL RESPONSIBILITY

Being on the birth certificate gives you Parental Responsibility (PR) even if you are unmarried. (Married fathers automatically have PR.) Otherwise, you must apply for it separately, with the mother's consent or see a solicitor. Without PR, a parent cannot authorize medical treatment for his or her child and does not have the right to see the child's medical records. PR means your child cannot be adopted without your agreement. Additionally it means that, even if you don't actually live with your child, you have to agree before your child's surname can be changed or before she can be taken out of the country for a significant period. So, it is *very* important to have.

I was shocked that the hospital could possibly let us take our tiny baby home, when I felt so totally clueless. The craziest things will go wrong at first: one father immediately blocked his drains by flushing nappies down the toilet. There is a lot to tackle – problems breastfeeding, sleeplessness, disorientation, going back to work. I remember thinking: "How come nobody warned us?"

WHAT'S IN A NAME?

Ever wondered why so many French men are called Antoine? Because the French only allow certain names and shout "non" at anything too fancy. In Britain, you can call your kids whatever you like, though one registrar did turn away parents who wanted to call their son "Save all the whales, here's a shiny balloon". The rules:

- You must register the baby within 42 days. Your local council has details of your nearest registration service.

- Dads married before the birth can register the baby by themselves (lots do), though if you give the child a crazy name, heaven help you when you get home.

- If you're not married then you have to go with the mother to register the birth. But if you are away and not able to accompany her, she can put your name on the certificate provided you sign a form saying she can.

- If you miss the boat, don't despair. It's never too late. One dad got his name on his daughter's birth certificate when she was 30.

- If you marry after the birth, get the birth certificate changed to protect your child's rights of inheritance.

Quality time

This time is for you, your partner, and your baby. Don't delay taking paternity leave – indeed, consider taking further (possibly unpaid) leave, if you can afford it. Suggest that your mother-in-law comes to stay in a few weeks, not right away.

Be supportive

You'll be amazed how much there is to do with a small baby that sleeps most of the time. And your partner needs you, especially if she has had a Caesarean or, around day three, when the often tearful "baby blues" may hit her for a day or two, as her body adjusts after pregnancy.

Your role

The next few weeks are vital to how you and your partner work together in the long run. Will you share child raising or treat her as "top parent" and regard yourself as her helper? Maybe you feel useless and unsure about your role, particularly when a breastfed baby focuses mainly on his mother. But you can still wind, settle, change, and bath him. Breastfed babies often settle better with dad as they are not distracted by the smell of mum's milk. At this point, when you are both learning together, you can prove to yourself that you can do all those things your dad probably never even tried.

POSTNATAL DEPRESSION

Postnatal depression can happen to a lot of women and should not be confused with the "baby blues", which lasts for only a few days. It is hard to distinguish from exhaustion but if your partner is really irritable, tearful, finding it very difficult to cope, and is sluggish, then it could be postnatal depression. Take as much responsibility for your baby as possible to give your partner breathing space. Talk to the health visitor and make sure she sees her GP. And find a friend to talk to yourself – it will help you cope.

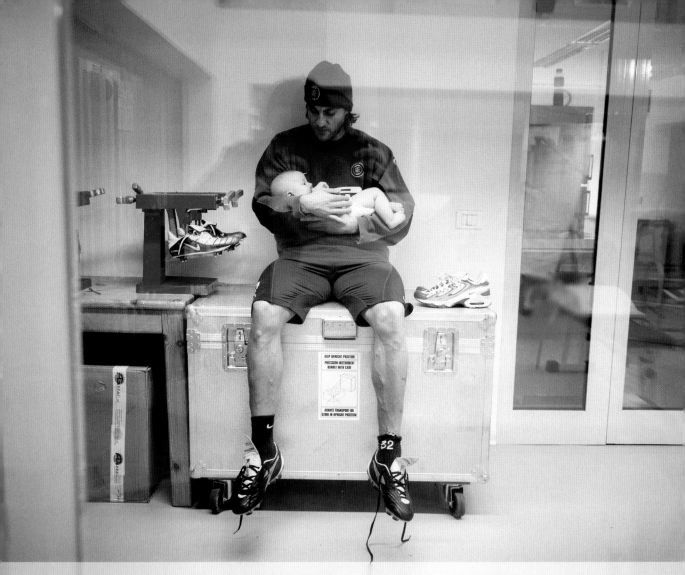

Settling into **fatherhood**

What do dads do? Trust your instincts. Pick up ideas from other dads. They gave me good tips about how the more I did, the more natural it feels. That's true. Change his nappy often; settle him to sleep; as often as you can, be the one who goes to him when he wakes; be alone occasionally with your baby to grow your confidence. Don't always drive – sit in the back with him.

10 ways to keep your baby healthy

Babies are tough – they must be to survive new parents. Yours has already been on a journey before you ever even held her in your arms. But babies are also vulnerable, particularly to rough treatment and when they are sleeping.

1 Never shake him – it can cause irreversible brain damage. Support his neck well, when lifting him.

2 Be extra careful with your baby's head: the fontanelle (tissue on the top of the head) remains soft and vulnerable to damage for the first year.

3 Stop smoking – or smoke outside. Your baby's health can be damaged by people smoking nearby.

4 Encourage your partner to breastfeed. Breastfed babies develop stronger defences against infection and are less likely to develop illnesses such as asthma.

5 Put your baby to sleep on her back, not on her front. Don't allow her to over-heat (*see panel right*).

6 Learn about maternal postnatal illness. It can impact not only on your partner but also on your baby.

7 Buy a good baby car seat – one that really supports him when sleeping.

8 When bathing your baby, dip your elbow into the water to test that it is not too hot.

9 Trust your own instincts if you think she is ill and seek professional help – babies can become very ill, very quickly.

10 If you are feeling low or unconfident, talk about it and ask for support from family and friends. Looking after yourself is good for your baby, too.

COT DEATH: FACTS AND PREVENTION

- Always put your baby down to sleep on her back. Studies show that putting your baby to sleep this way significantly lowers the risk of Sudden Infant Death Syndrome (SIDS or cot death). Once she is older, she will be able to turn herself onto her stomach. However, even then, carry on putting her to sleep on her back even if she does change position during the night.

- Never smoke around your baby – babies exposed to cigarette and cigar smoke are at higher risk of cot death.

- Don't over-heat your baby or his room. As yet, he cannot regulate his own body temperature properly. To test if he is too hot, feel his bare tummy or the nape of his neck.

- Place her feet at the end of the cot, Moses basket, or cradle. This is vital because it prevents your baby slipping under the covers and suffocating.

- Make sure babysitters also follow all of these instructions.

Breastfeeding:
what you need to know

Isn't breastfeeding the one part of this new life that is nothing to do with you? Wrong. You can make the difference between success and failure. It doesn't mean wearing a pair of false boobs – just give your partner good back up. Some dads even have a taste themselves!

1 Breast milk is the perfect food, providing all the nutrients a baby needs in the right quantities, for the first six months.

2 It's the healthiest option for babies. Breastfed, they have a lower risk of gastroenteritis; respiratory, urinary tract, and ear infections; eczema; and early-onset diabetes.

3 Adults who were breastfed as babies have IQs 5.2 points higher than those who were bottle-fed according to the American Journal of Clinical Nutrition.

4 Breastfed babies are less likely to be obese as adults.

5 It's convenient, instantly available, and always at the right temperature.

6 It's environmentally friendly – produced and delivered to the consumer without any pollution, unnecessary packaging, or waste.

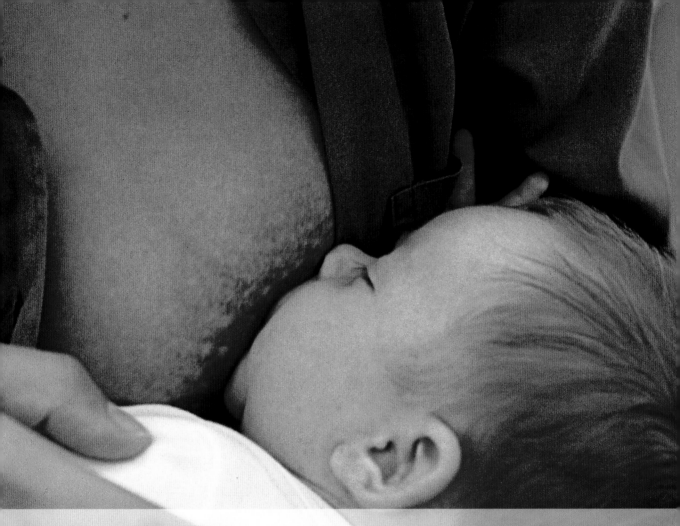

7 It's free – indeed it saves a family an estimated £450 across the baby's first year.

8 A mother who breastfeeds her baby has a lower risk of pre-menopausal breast cancer and ovarian cancer.

9 Women who breastfeed regain their figures sooner than women who bottle-feed – when a woman's body is making breast milk, it burns about 500 extra calories a day.

10 Remember, sometimes it doesn't work and sometimes it's terribly painful. Don't let your partner beat herself up over this. She can only do her best.

lifeafterbirth

It's time for the big push – swapping your dream of a Ferrari for a **baby in a cool buggy**. You'll find yourself wearing dark glasses at work after a **hard night's winding**, wiping his sick from your shoulder, swimming in the shallow end with your beautiful child, **singing him to sleep** and drifting off too. And you'll be thinking: "Will she ever come back to me – or always be too tired?"…"Can I muster the energy in any case?"… **"Wow, we're a family!"** But don't even think of having another one…yet.

Going **back to work**

You've just taken on a second job – you're moonlighting. So the trick, for now anyway, is to avoid big responsibilities or additional workloads in your money-earning job. It isn't easy. Most employers think that child care is for women only. They are oblivious to the fact that dads actually look after their kids. It's especially difficult in the early days when sleeplessness may leave you feeling like a zombie. Don't fret – no one else notices.

Treading water

Initially, you won't just be exhausted. You'll feel like you are doing neither the fathering nor the job properly. But remember, you're doing brilliantly if you just manage. You might tread water at work for a while, but there's plenty of time later to put in fresh energy. Remember you are of unique importance to your child, so postpone after-work wind-downs – particularly drinking – until after she is asleep.

Her career

Support your partner's career. If you end up doing all the breadwinning, she'll fall behind in career progress. The economics will drive you into longer hours and her into doing most of the child raising. Do either of you really want this?

Unemployment

What if you're out of work? Does that mean you're failing as a dad? Absolutely not. Just as mothers who are not in paid employment can make great parents, so can dads. Unemployment can affect your confidence, but don't let it stop you being there for your kids. A study of children from disadvantaged backgrounds who had done unusually well in life found that several had unemployed fathers – dads who had been closely involved in caring for, and supporting, them.

YOUR LAST 50 PACES HOME

So, you're feeling shattered and looking forward to a shower, a drink, and sympathy after what your boss said to you today. Forget it. Once that door opens, you'll probably have a baby shoved into your arms by a rather tired, grumpy mother, acting as though you've been down the pub with your mates all day. So, 50 paces from home, remember how stress can make you angry and cold with your child – and your partner. Once you've realized this, catch yourself and stop it. Take a few deep breaths, think about your family, and leave all the difficulties of your day behind. If you're still not ready, then walk around the block again until you are.

FITTING IT ALL IN

- Take shorter lunch times and breaks so you spend less time at work.

- Be ruthless about after-work socializing. Does the job really demand it? If not, go home.

- Start work earlier, so you can go home earlier. That might mean going to bed earlier, but your child will be up with the larks, so you can have time with him before work and still be back for bath time.

- Try, if you can, to work from home, even half a day a week, or flexibly, staying one evening a week in return for an afternoon. It's great to have time every week when you're the one in charge of your child.

- Don't imagine you'll get back into family life later, when you're "not so busy at work". By then, your family may have little in common with you. Act now.

Make sure you **stay involved**

It's easy to become detached. Work makes few concessions to fatherhood. "Mother and Baby" signs suggest you're not needed. Your inner voice says "I'm no good at this" or "she does it better". But ask yourself: "Am I going to be a modern man or a clone of an outdated, discredited stereotype?"

Health visitors

Start with the health visitor, who will come to your house every few days after the birth to check everything is alright. She's there to make sure your baby and partner are thriving. But her job includes helping you to make a successful transition into fatherhood. So when she visits, don't disappear into another room. Be there. Introduce yourself. Listen to her, learn, and feel free to raise any of your own concerns.

Your antenatal group

If you're back at work and your partner is meeting during the day with mums from the antenatal group, suggest they all come to your home one evening – with the dads. You'll feel much better when you've had a chance to catch up and compare the experiences of other families.

Baby time

Remember, even with a busy job, you can still be a great dad if you are ready to devote the rest of your time – mornings and evenings – to your child. The weekend offers huge opportunities. As does night-time, if you are prepared to go through the sleeplessness and be with your baby. It's all possible, but it's tough, tiring, and challenging. It needs self-discipline. You have to put your baby first and stop thinking too much about yourself for a while.

Volunteer for everything

Your baby needs to go to the doctor. Offer to take her. Who's going to sleep next to the cot? You're willing to – at least some nights. There's shopping to be done, take the baby too. Bring her into work. Show her to colleagues. Confront those parts of your life that currently have the stamp: "no-go area for children".

JUST YOU AND YOUR BABY

Yes, go for a pint (just the one). Why wait until he's 18? Start at six weeks, provided it isn't smoky. Dominoes, crisps, and a lemonade can follow in a year or two. Swimming is great for a hangover, or put him in the sling and head for the swings. He'll love it. Bunk off with him on Saturday mornings to a Dads' Club. Go baby clothes shopping. Or let your partner go out, while you two stay in, chat, and play.

Ball juggling:
how different dads cope

It's not just women who struggle to balance professional life and parenting. Modern dads typically work longer hours than before fatherhood, while spending more time than ever with their kids.

Home dad

Keith McLean, a film extra, became a home dad when his partner, Catherine, went back to work 14 weeks after Izaac was born:

"We realized that Catherine could earn enough working part-time to keep us, so she went back when Izaac was 14 weeks old. It wasn't easy. Days on can be 14 hours long and sometimes she is away a week at a time. But I was happy. By then I had changed him many times and I knew how he needed to be fed, so I was running on instinct.

"It could be stressful if he didn't eat or he threw up. He would be crying, scared. There was the mess to clear up on my own. At night, the key was being prepared, preparing a bottle so I did not have to mix one when I was half asleep and he was crying in my arms. I had a change of clothing, nappies, and creams, so everything was on hand if he was ill. It was like a military operation. I would go to bed as early as possible because I knew I would be woken at least three times.

"He was ill a couple of times while Catherine was away. It's always worrying when a baby has a temperature and does not want to eat. It is important to know where the baby paracetamol is and how to read a thermometer and how high a child's temperature should be.

"I look on that time very positively. I have learned an enormous amount about Izaac. Children teach you patience. And I have learned how to do many things in one day. Fortunately, because we joined an NCT group, I never became isolated. I had a network that was always on the end of the phone. I know it may seem scary to be responsible like this for a baby, but once you get stuck in, the enjoyment outweighs your fears."

IZAAC

I look on that time very positively. I have learned an enormous amount about Izaac

Sharing dad

John Callen, a furniture-maker, shares the care of Siena (two), and Maya (six), with Pam, a painter:

"Up until now it has worked really well. Whenever one of us has had a particular deadline or a lot of work on, the other has had the flexibility to take over responsibility for the children. The rest of the time, we share the jobs. I'll do the lunch boxes, Pam gets Maya up, I'll dress Siena. I'll take them to nursery or school and Pam picks them up.

"It tends to work best when one or the other is not around. If we are both there when the children are tired, then Siena will go into a crying fit, Maya might start up, and everything deteriorates. It just seems to work better when one of us is in charge.

"I would not want to look after the children all the time. I'd find that difficult and so would Pam. She needs to paint. If she goes any time without painting she gets fractious. Then again, she feels guilty if she isn't looking after the children. But it seems to help her much more if I'm looking after them – it's psychological. Maybe she knows they are safe when I have them.

"It's great fun if you accept that part of your job is looking after children. The frustration comes if you know there is another job you really need to do and you can't get at it."

Changed dad

Richard Wigley, a carpenter, missed out on his first family. Second time around, he is not making the same mistake:

"When I was a child, I hardly ever saw my dad. He felt his role was to work as hard as he could and bring in the money. We never saw him. So when I became a dad, I did the same and my wife looked after the kids.

"Sometimes, I'd be abroad working for six weeks at a time. One week off didn't make up for the lost time with

She asked: "Where were you, dad, all those years?"

the children. It was no good for the kids. And work killed my marriage.

"I try to make it up to my children, but what can you do? My daughter is at university now. She rang me up one day and just asked, "Where were you, dad, all those years?" We spent an hour on the phone. I wanted to cry. We talked and we're a lot closer. But it still tears me up.

"Now, I'm with a wonderful partner, Carol, and we have a lovely daughter, Eliza. I am with Eliza probably 70 per cent of the time. I love being with her, seeing her growing up, cooking for her, having time to play with her, putting her to bed. I wish I could have done this for my first family."

Trad dad

Michael Jackson is a database administrator and lives with Ruth, a surveyor, and their children, Robbie (14 weeks), Kily (21 months), and Fionn (11), Ruth's son from a previous relationship:

"It seems logical that I'm at work while Ruth is at home, especially as she's still breastfeeding Robbie. I get home about 6pm and I look after Kily, bath him, and put him to bed. I'd definitely like more quality time. If I get in late, Kily is tired and it's a big rush to get him into bed. I tried getting up at 6.30am and leaving before the children woke up, so I could get home by 4.30pm or 5pm, but Kily would wake up, I'd give him his breakfast, look at the clock, and realize I wasn't going to get to work early enough.

"I'd like more flexibility, maybe have some time off work, while Ruth goes back, and I'd look after the kids. But we'll have to wait a while until my work gets more predictable and Ruth is ready. Maybe, she could work two days and I could work two days. Until then I have to make up time at the weekends, catching up with the children. It's OK. I ring four or five times a day from work. But I don't want it to be like this forever."

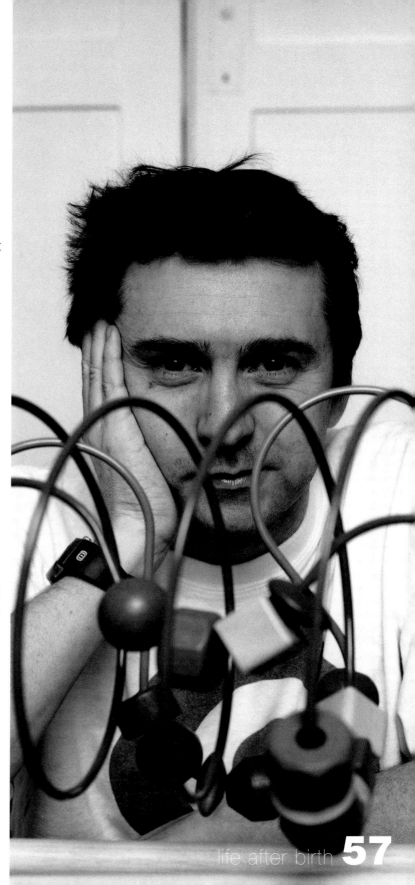

Young fathers

As a young dad you may feel up against it – frequently dismissed as irresponsible, possibly without a job, money, or your own home in which to house mother and baby. Your relationship with your baby's mother may be rocky; perhaps it had hardly got going before she became pregnant. Yet, you are as important to your child as any dad – and you can be a great success.

Breaking the stereotype

Pat Anderson, a Bristol University researcher, studies young dads and has found that a lot of stereotypes are untrue. She talks about Brian, who was 17 when his girlfriend, Katy, became pregnant with their son, Jimmy. "In the space of less than a year he matured amazingly," says Pat. "He passed his driving test, got a new job more suitable to his responsibilities, and was saving money. We tend to think of young

> We are going to have to grow up pretty quickly, but I respect that.

fatherhood as pushing men out of the mainstream. But, in many cases, it is quite the opposite. Many are keen to make it work."

Growing up fast

Brian explains: "Obviously, there is still a part of me that thinks I'm young. But I've got to be prepared not to see my mates and not spend my money at the start of the month and then have nothing for the rest. With a baby you can't do that. You've got to make sure there is enough in the bank, so we are going to have to grow up pretty quickly, but I respect that. There is someone going to be calling me, 'Daddy', you know."

The key to success

So what is the secret of being a successful young dad? The first is the same as for all fathers – do your best to support, care for, and get on with your child's mother, whether or not you live together or still have a romantic relationship. But it is particularly important if you are a young dad and a lot of other people give you the impression that you don't matter in your child's life. You need your partner, ex or otherwise, to believe that you can improve her life and that of the child you have together. That doesn't necessarily mean working all hours to pay for everything. It also means being an able, competent, reliable parent, who can free her up, for example, to carry on an education that might have been cut short by her pregnancy.

Family and friends

The second key ingredient is trying to recruit your family and friends to help you out, especially if you are separated. Raising a child is an awesome task, but it's even tougher when you are alone, perhaps with poor housing and little cash. Also remember, when your child is older and you are friends, still in the prime of your life, you won't regret what might, at times, have seemed like a terrible mistake that would ruin your life.

Essential **baby kit**

They arrive with nothing. In no time, they need a truck load of gear to go anywhere and your home becomes full of strange bottles, creams, and lotions. Yet, you still can't find any shampoo.

Staying In

Nappies
Wipes
Antiseptic cream
Baby gros
Jumpers
Vests
Sleepsuit
Sheets
Blanket
Thermometer
Towels
Sterilizing solution
Cot
Moses basket
Highchair
Nappy bin
Music system
Baby alarm
Baby gym
Any-way-up cup
Baby bath or baby-shaped
    sponge support
Sterilizing kit (if bottle-feeding)
Changing mat
Wine (for you)
DVDs (for you)

Going Out

Warm jumpsuit
Hat
Buggy – adjustable so she can
    sleep in it
Blanket
Thermometer
Gloves
Changing bag and mat
Car seat
Travel cot
Sling
Car bottle and food warmer
Mobile phone

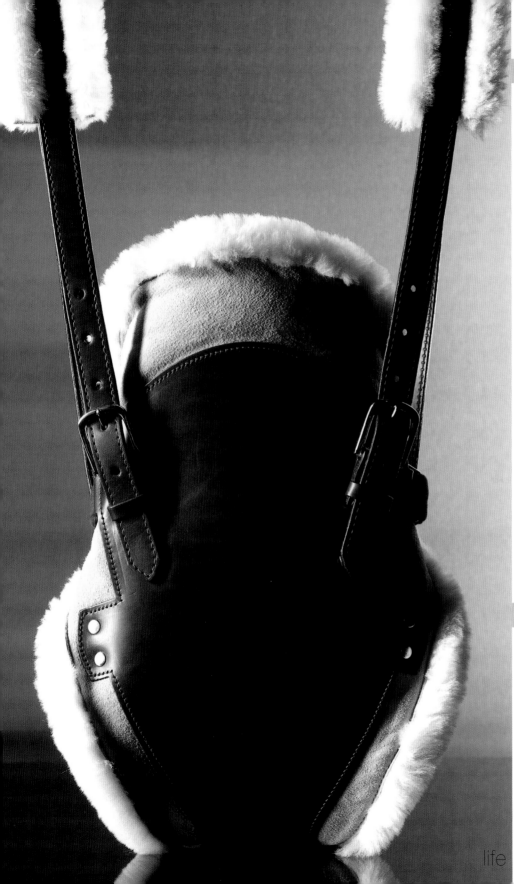

FOETAL FAN

Leicester City fans, Jack Summerfield and his wife, Sandra, were so keen to recruit their child to the football cause, they registered their daughter Georgina for a season ticket with the club ten weeks after conceiving her. The Leicester City fanatics handed over an ultrasound scan for the photograph on her membership card.

life after birth **61**

Bonding time

Men are not usually expected to have close relationships with their babies. Yet, there is now a mass of academic research showing how sensitive dads are to their young children. So be confident and hands on.

Shared responses

You may be surprised to learn that there is no difference between the response patterns of men and women to their newborn babies. Research shows that both men and women experience increases in heart rate, blood pressure, and skin temperature when they see their baby smiling or crying. You can't tell the difference between mums and dads.

Father-baby bond

Babies usually bond as easily with their fathers as their mothers. Many studies have compared the ways in which one to two year olds relate to their parents and have found that closeness of father and baby is almost identical to that of mother and baby. This happens even when fathers have only a little time each day with the baby because of long working hours. How you spend time with your baby is more important to your relationship than how often you are with him. It is really vital that you do things like bathing, changing nappies, playing, and putting him to bed.

Main carer

Also bear in mind that there are many men who actually become the main carer for a baby very early on. Maybe your partner is unwell after the birth, recovering from a Caesarean section or experiencing postnatal depression, for example. Indeed, if your partner is depressed, then it is very important that you spend plenty of time with your baby.

Trust your instincts

All of this research is particularly interesting because it covers decades when there was virtually no education for fathers in early parenting. It shows that we have huge capacities within ourselves, just as mothers do. We don't need a lot of people to tell us what to do. We can trust ourselves.

Physio for babies

You can massage your baby from about two weeks. Best in a warm room and when he isn't sleepy. Big hands (make sure they are warm) can help a baby feel secure.

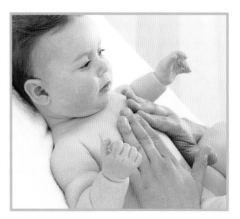

1 Start with his head, gently massaging his crown, forehead, and cheeks using circular strokes. Give him plenty of eye contact and lots of smiles and kisses.

2 Move to his neck, shoulders, and arms, then his chest and tummy, using a light downward motion. Talk to him or sing if you prefer.

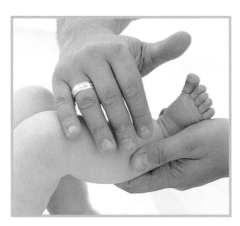

3 Next, massage his legs, stroking downwards from his thighs to his knees, then around his shins and ankles, gently squeezing them as you go.

4 Finally, stroke his feet from heel to toe, then gently massage each toe. This process draws any tension out of his body.

Feeding baby

If your baby is bottle-fed, there is plenty for you to do. You can be great at feeding: research shows that dads respond sensitively when a baby wants to pause or splutter, and that the baby takes just as much milk from dad as from mum.

Bottle-feeding

Feeding your baby with a bottle can be a real pleasure both for your baby and for you. It is an opportunity for the two of you to get really tuned into each other. Cuddling her and giving her good attention is key to the whole experience. Always hold her close to you, smile at her, and talk to her. She will soon look up at you quite attentively while you are feeding her.

Your baby's in control

Give your baby as much control over feeding as possible. She should set the pace, feel able to stop, and touch the bottle. You'll soon get a sense of how long she takes to finish the feed. Let her decide when she has had enough and don't push her to take more. Never leave your baby alone with a bottle – she could choke.

The switch to solids

Between the ages of three and six months, your baby will be ready to try solid food. No sirloin steaks yet, but a bit of sweet-potato puree or mashed apple will slip down easily. You will know the time because, after a full feed, he still seems hungry. You can gradually build in more and more solid foods until by a year or so your baby may wean himself off the breast.

Healthy habits

Give him as many new foods as possible (not too much sugary or salty food), but if he turns them away, don't have a confrontation. Just present them again at a later date. If you want your child to eat healthily in the long run, then make sure that in the early years you don't make food a battleground.

WINDING

This is an important job for a dad, who might be called for duty at any time of the day or night. To help a very young baby bring up wind, put her against your shoulder and rub her back, or lean her forwards on your lap, supporting her floppy head under the chin. She's very likely to bring up some milk. Alternatively, you can hold your baby face down across your lap or in your arms and rub her back. When she's older, say three months, you can sit her up on your lap, rubbing her back so she can burp swallowed air.

ALLERGIES

Food allergies are increasingly common, caused when the body's immune system overreacts. Symptoms might be slight – flushing skin, eczema, mild hives on the body, itchiness, and runny eyes. However with severe allergy, known as anaphylaxis, the condition becomes acute rapidly and is life-threatening.

With anaphylaxis, the throat, mouth, and lung tissue can swell, making it hard for the baby to breath. She may vomit. Blood pressure drops, and collapse and unconsciousness may follow quickly. It can happen in babies as they are weaned from breast to cow's milk or onto new foods. Call an ambulance and seek medical help.

The most common foods to cause an allergic reaction are peanuts and tree nuts, soya, sesame, fish, milk, eggs, and dairy products. Mild symptoms are treated with an oral antihistamine. But a severe reaction may need an injection of adrenalin, which acts to restore blood pressure, improve breathing, stimulate the heartbeat, and stop swelling.

COLIC

You will know if your baby has colic, which typically occurs in the evenings, from about three weeks until about three months. It is characterized by intense, inconsolable screaming, possibly for several hours and can be very tough for everyone. There is no cure but time, and all you can do is to try to sooth your baby as much as possible, keeping him in motion, offering him regular feeds, and rubbing his stomach.

The joy of **nappies**

There is a lot of nonsense spoken about men, poo, and nappies, as if it is all a great mystery to us. You – and your partner – may gag at changing other children's nappies, but it feels OK with your own baby. You will, however, be stunned at the amazing array of colours and consistencies your baby produces on a simple diet. Nappy chat is endless.

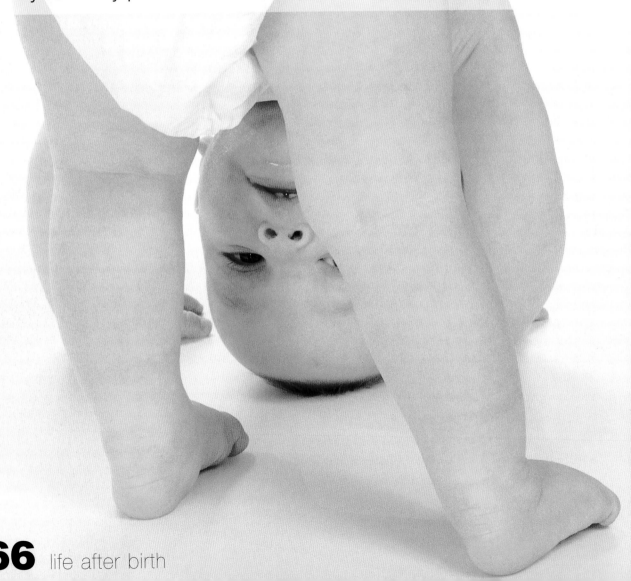

How to change a nappy

As soon as you smell the warning signs, get cracking to avoid nuclear fall-out and a complete clothes change. You'll need warm water and cotton wool or baby wipes.

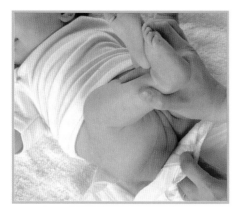

1 Lift your baby gently by the ankles, and remove the dirty nappy. Never dispose of nappies down the toilet.

2 Wipe between your baby's leg creases and genitals. With girls, wipe from front to back, to avoid infecting her vagina.

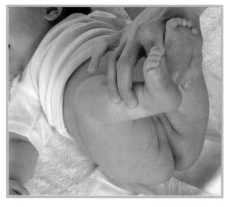

3 Thoroughly dry your baby's bottom to help avoid nappy rash. (If a rash develops, slap on antiseptic cream.) Next, slide a clean nappy underneath her.

4 Disposable nappies are easy to secure. Simply lift the front of the nappy up to her stomach and secure with the sticky tabs at the sides – just not too tightly.

BOTTOMS UP

- Your baby is champion in the pooing department, needing maybe ten nappies a day. Grimaces normally indicate another Herculean effort.

- Never leave your baby out of your reach when changing his nappy. It's easy for him to roll and hurt himself.

- Always wash your hands thoroughly after changing a nappy.

NAPPY MOUNTAIN

Most disposable nappies are not biodegradable and the 4,000 that your baby will use in his lifetime could, if dumped, leave a bigger mess than a large herd of nervous elephants, for a period of 200 years. Cloth nappies, combined with disposable paper and cotton linings, are one answer. They can be a bit of a pain to wash, though there are excellent cleaning services available. It all needs a bit of commitment from both of you. As women seem to think that men are genetically programmed to do the bins, perhaps this is something you could lead on. "No way!" OK... just a thought.

Rub-a-**dub-dub**

Bath time is dad time. It's an opportunity to relax your baby before bed. Why not climb in too? It's a bit of a change from getting into the shower with the boys after the match…certainly much colder.

Finding confidence

Hopefully, a midwife helped you bath your baby soon after the birth. It's all about being organized, holding him confidently, then wrapping him up in a warm towel. You'll get into a routine that is relaxing and familiar. As he gets older, you will know his favourite toys, how he likes to be held, and games he likes to play.

Essential bath kit

First, make sure your kit is ready: baby bath or non-slip mat, baby bath wash and lotion, a thick warm towel, a clean nappy, and a change of clothes. If bathing him in your tub, you can buy a sponge, baby-shaped rest to place underneath him for extra support.

How to wash your baby

Support your baby's neck and head with one hand, put the other underneath his bottom and upper part of his legs, then lower him into your tub slowly. Chat to him calmly. Once he is settled, let his bottom and legs rest on the base of the bath and use your free hand to wash him. Then lift him out for drying and a cuddle.

You'll soon get into a routine that is relaxing and familiar

DO

- Test the water with your elbow, (it's more sensitive than your hand), to ensure it's not too hot. A thermometer should register about 29°C (85°F).

- Try getting in as well. Hold him, face up, with his head against your knees and legs pointing towards your stomach.

DON'T

- Leave her unattended. Babies may feel at home in water, but it's a dangerous place for them.

- Fill your bath too deep. It should be about 13cm (5in) deep. Don't let the taps run while he is in the tub in case it suddenly gets hot.

- Wear flippers.

Sleep easy

Dads have some advantages when it comes to getting babies to the Land of Nod. Unlike mums, we don't smell of milk. And often we've not been with the baby all day, so we may be fresher and calmer.

AGONY UNCLE

Q: How long should our baby sleep?

A: In the first six weeks, your baby will be awake for only six to eight hours a day. Sadly, it's usually when you want to sleep. From then until three months, she will sleep less in the day and more at night. By six months, she will, typically, be able to sleep in four-hour stretches at night between feeds. From then on, she should manage six-hour stretches and, with luck, you're pretty much into a good routine.

A quiet time to bond

Sleeplessness in babies – and therefore adults – is considered the great problem of early parenthood. It leaves you tired and grumpy, and messes up work the next day. Yet, in the depth of the night, when one of our children is awake and it's just me and him or her, it doesn't always feel like a problem. Sometimes, it is a wonderful private time, when all the clutter of the day is set aside and I can take care of them without anything interrupting us. Being there, undistracted, albeit jaded, creates a terrific bond between us that's still there as they grow up.

Get into a routine

Bedtime routine is vital, signalling to your baby that it's time for sleep and helping her wind down. Bath, night clothes, feed (in a dimly lit bedroom), cuddle, and bed is a good schedule. Put your baby to sleep on her back. Don't over-heat her or cover her head: place her feet at the bottom of the cot, so the bedding cannot ride up (*see "Cot Death: Facts and Prevention" p.45*).

What if he won't go to sleep?

Some experts advise the Ferber method. It does work and rarely takes more than a week – but it can be tough. You put your baby into the cot when he's still awake. You leave him there and, if he cries, return to reassure him every five minutes until eventually he falls asleep. You have to be utterly consistent to carry this method through.

Scheduled awakenings

For babies that wake up regularly at a certain hour of the night, scheduled awakenings are recommended. So if your baby wakes around 1am, then, on night one, wake him 15 minutes early. Once the baby learns to wait for you to wake him up, you can push back the waking time in 15-minute increments.

Ten tips for contented nights

There are two key issues: first, getting your baby to sleep and, second, keeping her there. It's often the first that is, by far, the easiest.

1 Stick to a bedtime routine so that your baby is familiar with all the signals that say she should be going to sleep.

2 Try not to let him get over-tired. Best to catch him with a lullaby as the first wave of sleepiness passes over him.

3 You could try putting her in your bed with you. It makes breastfeeding simpler, offering, at first, less broken nights. But you must make sure it is safe for your baby (see points 4 and 5).

4 If you opt for three in a bed, he should be up by your heads, covered by light blankets, not a duvet.

5 Always, for safety reasons, put her in a cot if you've been drinking, smoking, taking any medication, or are especially tired. Don't share if the bed is cramped.

6 Put the baby in another, quieter room. This is possible after six months and once he is having longer intervals between feeds. A baby alarm allows monitoring.

7 Babies are often comforted to sleep by the familiar smell of a soft cloth – often a muslin cloth that is used during feeds – or a particular toy.

8 Dummies are sometimes useful in helping your baby to fall asleep on her own.

9 Throw a soft towel over your shoulder to give the baby something to nestle against if walking her to sleep. Try singing – at worst it will bore her to sleep.

10 Make sure that your baby falls asleep in the room in which he is going to spend the night. Otherwise, he may wake up confused and upset.

Save your baby!

With many dads now doing between 30 and 40 per cent of the parental childcare for the under-fives, it is crucial that fathers know about the major risks to their children and how to deal with them in an emergency. Even if you are rarely alone with your baby, knowledge can still save her life.

Meningitis

Symptoms: fever; listlessness; vomiting; loss of appetite; headache or, in babies, a slightly tense fontanelle; pain in the eyes from light; stiffness in neck; convulsions; a rash of red or purple spots. Call a doctor urgently.

Fitting

Symptoms: baby may be very hot, eyes rolling, turning blue, arched back, clenching fists. Undress him to his nappy, and pad the area around the child to protect him from injury. Open a window or use an electric fan to ensure a free flow of cool air over the baby's skin. (Be careful, however, not to let him get too cold.) When the convulsions stop, roll him on his side, keeping his head tilted back. Cover him with a sheet and call a doctor.

Choking

Signs: breathing obstructed, face turning blue, making strange noises or trying to cry but making no noise. Lay your baby face down with

A GUIDE TO JABS

Babies must get used to being jabbed with needles from a very early age. Their first three injections are given at two, three, and four months of age, each a combination of five vaccines against diphtheria, polio, tetanus, whooping cough, and Hib (a bacterium that can cause meningitis). In each of those visits, a dose of the single meningitis C vaccine is given in a single jab. At 12–15 months, infants are offered the combined MMR vaccine against measles, mumps, and rubella. Age three to five, they can receive a pre-school MMR booster and a separate booster against diphtheria, tetanus, whooping cough, and polio.

her head low along your forearm. Support her head and shoulders on your hand. Give five sharp slaps to the upper part of her back. Scoop her mouth with one finger to check for obstruction. If slapping fails, lay your baby on her back, place two fingers on the lower half of her breastbone, just below the level of her nipples, and thrust upwards five times at a rate of one every three seconds. If this is not successful, repeat the whole process twice more. If the blockage has still not cleared, take your baby with you and call an ambulance.

Heavy bleeding

Press firmly on the wound with a pad or handkerchief to stop the bleeding. Lay the child down and keep the injured part above the heart. If the bleeding doesn't stop, raise his legs and support them on cushions. Call an ambulance, but do not leave the child unattended. Loosen his clothing and keep him warm.

Severe allergy

Anaphylactic shock may occur following an injection of a drug, an insect sting, or eating particular food, such as nuts. Signs: difficulty breathing, swelling of the face and neck, red blotchy skin, rapid pulse, unconsciousness. Clear the mouth. If the child is known to be allergic, administer her medication. Call an ambulance. Help the child sit in a position that eases her breathing.

Unconsciousness

Check for a response – tap the sole of the foot. Never shake a baby. Shout for help. Open the airway – place the baby on her side and support her chin with two fingers (but do not tilt the head). Look in her mouth and remove any obstructions with your finger.

Check for breathing for up to 10 seconds (listen, look for chest movement, feel for breath on your cheek). If she's not breathing, seal your lips tightly around your baby's mouth and nose and breathe gently into the lungs until the chest rises. Then remove your lips and let the chest fall back. Continue to ventilate for five breaths.

Check for a pulse on the inside of her arm midway between the shoulder and elbow. Feel for up to 10 seconds. If a pulse is present, but the baby is still not breathing, repeat artificial ventilation at 20 breaths per minute, take your baby with you to call an ambulance, and then continue artificial ventilation until help arrives.

If there is no pulse, place your baby on a firm surface. Place the tips of your two fingers on her lower breastbone just below the nipple line. Press down sharply to a depth of 1–2 centimetres. Do this five times, at about 100 compressions per minute (slightly quicker than one per second). Then give one full breath of artificial ventilation. Continue this cycle of five chest compressions and one breath of ventilation until an ambulance arrives.

Mapping out
the first year

The first twelve months are amazing – particularly for your baby. In the beginning, he will be oblivious to his surroundings. By a year, he may be saying his first words, playing with a ball, and be deeply attached to you. Remember that "normal" covers a wide range: babies develop at different rates.

PHYSICAL

By six months, your baby will probably:

- Stick out his tongue and open his mouth in imitation of you.
- Bring his hands to his mouth and hold them together. Use his hands to explore his face and objects of interest.
- Keep his head steady; grab his toes and put them in his mouth.
- Roll from his stomach onto his back and then onto his stomach again.
- Clasp a rattle and raise his arms to be picked up.

And by 12 months...

- Sit up unsupported and begin to crawl.
- Pull herself up to a standing position and edge around a room, holding on to furniture.
- Stand momentarily unsupported.
- Feed herself finger foods.
- Be able to walk a couple of steps on her own.

DAD'S JOURNEY

It's a whirlwind: total involvement with the birth and during paternity leave and then, for the typical dad, back to work as though nothing has happened. But there's still lots of time to marvel at your child's development. You can test your newborn's reflexes. Stroke her cheek and her mouth will try to suck. Hold her upright with feet touching a surface and she will lift each foot as

INTELLECTUAL

By six months your baby will probably:

- Show excitement when she knows you are near.

- Gurgle.

- Recognize people closest to her as individuals and have a distinct reaction to different voices.

- Blow bubbles and "raspberries".

- Know that she can get attention by making sounds and banging objects.

And by 12 months...

- Say "dada" and "mama" – but he may not say it to the right person until later.

- Wave hello and goodbye.

- Know that he is a separate person from a parent.

- Play pat-a-cake and peek-a-boo.

- Play with a ball and start to understand how objects are used – for example, listening to a telephone and drinking from a cup.

- Utter his first word (other than "mama" and "dada".)

SOCIAL AND EMOTIONAL

By six months, your baby will probably:

- Smile and laugh with pleasure when you talk or smile at him.

- Begin to say vowel sounds ("ooh-ooh-ooh") in response to you talking or smiling.

- Be very attached to you and cry when you leave him. Be anxious about strange situations.

- Want to be included in everything.

- Turn his head when he doesn't want any more food.

And by 12 months...

- Enjoy imitating people.

- Be anxious about strangers.

- Be wary of situations that were once OK.

- Respond to simple commands. Use gestures, such as shaking her head at you when wanting to say "no".

- Recognize her name and other familiar words like "hello".

if to walk. Tap your baby's nose and both eyes will close. During the first few months, communicate through physical closeness. Touch stimulates the brain to release hormones necessary for growth. Talk, read, and sing – she is beginning to learn about language from the sounds you use and the tone of your voice, even when she does not understand words.

Try being a **home dad**

Back in the Seventies, John Lennon was one of the first home dads. Now, the numbers are doubling every five years. But the latest "dads' army" of fathers looking after the kids all day while mum is at work still seems exotic. For a start, what are they actually called? "Home dad" is increasingly popular, but sometimes it's "house husband", "full-time father", or "stay-at-home dad". Shoot anyone who calls you "Mr Mom".

HALAL FATHER

A man named Al-Aqra ibn Habis visited the Noble Prophet and was surprised to see him kiss his grandsons, Hassan and Hussein. "Do you kiss your children?" the man asked, adding that he had ten children and never kissed one of them. "[That shows] you have no mercy and tenderness at all. Those who do not show mercy to others will not have God's mercy shown on them," commented the Messenger of God.

Why do it?

Families make the choice for lots of reasons, but most of them are economic. Most people are short of cash when a baby comes along and if your partner earns more than you and has better career prospects, then it makes sense to reverse the traditional roles.

Be different

The rewards of staying at home are many, as lots of mums and home dads testify, but all the issues new mothers sometimes face – loss of confidence and isolation – can be multiplied for a home dad who may not have the supportive networks mothers enjoy. It helps if you are outgoing, don't mind being different, and enjoy the company of women.

Join the club

Nick Cavender, founder of the website *www.homedad.org.uk* says: "Group organizers are usually appreciative of anyone who offers to set up, put away toys, or make the tea; and quite a few dads end up as treasurer. Some fathers also take the initiative and set up a playgroup specifically for dads. But baby and toddler groups aren't the only activity on offer. I go to the gym a couple of mornings a week and so Phoebe goes to the crèche and does lots of crafts. We also go to the toy library, a musical group, and a baby-gym session."

Ups and downs of being a home dad

The world is only beginning to understand and recognize home dads. As any mother knows, the rewards are not public, but private – from your children.

1 Darren, ex-fireman, ponders the best bits after ditching his 60-hour-a-week job: "Take your pick: first smile, first crawl, first tooth, first walk, first words, first drawing…I was there for all of them."

2 Andrew, former systems analyst, recalls occasional confusions: "Very early on I was pushing the pram with my brother. A 10 year old pointed at us and said: 'Hey look, gay people'."

3 Karl likes animal stuff: "I can stomp like a bear, slither like a snake, and jump like a kangaroo. Best of all, I can see our boys develop into men, then, hopefully, they can look after me."

4 Stuart remembers his first Fathers' Day: "I was bought a deep-fat fryer. For once I would have preferred socks. But I would really like to be bought something very masculine like a rally driving or tank driving lesson."

5 Nick gets recognized: "A mother who recently joined the toddler group said it was daunting as she doesn't know anyone. At least as a dad everyone recognizes you the next time you go."

Pitaji

Appa

Ayya

Bapuji

Papi

Baba

Pop

AB

El Obuja

Papacito

Vater

Père

Da

Daddy

Tata

Father

Ntate

Vader

Papa

Reviving your **social life**

Remember when you were a teenager and couldn't understand why your parents were such sad specimens, glued to the TV every night with no friends and no social life. It may feel like the rot sets in with the birth. But there is life after babies.

Key things to do:

Maybe the days of raves till dawn and wild weekends are over – for now – but there are other ways to stay sane.

Get your friends round

Many of them will be in the same boat so if you can't all go out, stay in together. Babies and young children are mobile and will sleep anywhere.

Swim late at night

Most leisure centres stay open late, so you can eat, get the kids to bed, and still have time for a swim or some exercise in the gym. Take turns. It will keep both of you healthy and happy.

Buy a DVD player

OK, so you may give up reading film reviews on new releases for a few years – but you won't be too far behind, DVDs are out almost as fast.

Pick eager godparents

When choosing, go for the childless godparents who'll really want to spend quantity time with your children – alone while the two of you are out on the town.

Join a babysitting circle

Sounds vaguely spooky, but if you can swap babysitting shifts with other couples, it can be a whole lot more reassuring than opting in desperation for a 15 year old with a dodgy boyfriend.

BATTLE OF THE CREASES

Fathers in Crickhowell, mid-Wales, organized the first-ever World Ironing Championships. Acknowledging the well-known truth that it's men who are best at pressing, flattening, folding, and putting that "straight-from-the-packet" feel back into jaded, collar-frayed shirts, they unleashed their boards and took on local mums to see who could pile them highest. With high hopes of turning macho-ironing into an Olympic sport, this first steamy foray saw the Iron Ladies win the battle of the creases. But the dads say they are back in training again, ironing in front of TV repeats of *Desperate Housewives*, preparing for the next championships.

When the going **gets tough**

You've made a baby together, but can you keep your relationship going? For some people, it's not a problem. Having a child just brings them closer together. They tend to be people with few money worries and lots of help. They are often older and content with their choices.

Find lots to do together – watching TV, going for a walk, looking after the kids

But many couples break up within a few years of becoming parents. For all the joy of having a baby, this event comes with mixed emotions, including anger and a sense of loss. Maybe you have already split up, in which case it's just as important that you have a positive relationship with your ex-partner. Your baby needs to see plenty of both of you and will be better off if you get along well.

Spotting problems

Relationship expert Adrienne Burgess suggests a checklist to help you spot things going wrong early. Ask yourselves whether the relationship was wobbly even before the baby; if you didn't really want to be a parent; whether many other relationships or those of your parents have "failed"; if you feel lonely; if your sex life is at a standstill; or if your partner refuses to talk. Ask yourselves if one of you is highly critical, or tends to place blame, is physically hurting the other one, or is flirting with someone else. Adrienne suggests that if you or your partner say "that's me" to a few of these questions, then you may be heading for trouble and you should talk. You'll need to be able to listen to each other in a non-blaming way. And if you can't, if you keep rowing, then you should seek counselling help. It's not just for the two of you – though that's important – you have a baby to think of now as well.

Caring for her

Ensure that you both get real breaks – that each sleeps in or goes out. Listen, don't attack, when she gets angry. Find lots to do together – watching TV, going for a walk, looking after the kids.

SEX POST-BABY

Let's face it. Sex and babies don't really go together. For a start, there's three of you and it's not a *ménage à trois* that inspires hanky panky.

All your would-be breathless abandon is likely to be interrupted by one of you wondering, of that fragile little life nearby, "is he still breathing?" And then, there are the physical problems of sex after birth. I don't just mean disentangling that maternity bra. Your partner may have had a difficult delivery, stitches, feel unattractive. Medical advice demands a break – at least six weeks, probably more – and it may take your partner much longer to recover from the shock of birth. Be patient and loving. In a while, you'll engineer times when your baby is not nearby and you both have mental space. But for now, be patient and wait.

Tackling a
toddler

He still looks like a baby when he's wrapped up in the bath towel or asleep. But **he's walking, talking, shouting**, hiding, playing games with you, and laughing. She's **sitting at her own place at the table** not in a high chair, drinking from a cup not a bottle, out of her cot and into a bed. **"I can dress myself, Dad,"** as two feet appear out of one trouser leg, and shoes go on the wrong feet. **Suddenly, he's not around** for hours on end – he's with the child minder, **at nursery**, or out with friends. Independence beckons, **babyhood passes**.

Quick quiz
can you manage a toddler?

Has Slack Dad succumbed to the charms of potty training? Is Fun Dad still an enthusiast? Does nothing stop Super Dad loving every minute. Test yourself…

1 Complete this phrase: My toddler…

a ...keeps getting up at 6am, but building towers during the dawn chorus is brilliant fun.

b ...plays with me every evening before bed.

c ...would be best kept in a zoo.

2 When you hear the words, "She's growing up so fast", what comes to mind first?

a A slight melancholia, followed by a shrugging acceptance of the wonderful glories of the cycle of human existence.

b A mild sense of guilt at the relief you feel, knowing that one day you may have something left over to contribute to a pension scheme.

c A cunning plan to invent a growth-acceleration drug that makes children into adults within a week, if not faster.

3 After he tips his chocolate milkshake over your computer, do you:

a Say, "My poor little precious darling. Don't worry. There's another one in the fridge." ?

b Start shaking almost uncontrollably and suggest quietly that mum takes him outside for a while?

c Clean it up in the hope that you can get on the Internet to find out if anyone in China is looking to adopt from overseas?

4 Your mum says she'd like to have your two year old to stay for the weekend. Your response is:

a "I don't think it's possible. I wouldn't have anyone to take me to the playground and the train set really needs two for it to be fun."

b Delight. You pack his favourite books, best drinking cup for the night, and carefully talk your mum through his bedtime routine.

c You remind your partner not to forget to pack the handcuffs – your mum is in for a rough ride!

5 Your partner looks lovingly at newborn babies and you know what she's thinking. Do you:

a Say, "Time we got another one of those," in a gruff but loving manner?

b Put your arm around her, in a gruff but loving manner?

c Put your arm around her, saying you're late for golf and you'll be back around 9 for dinner?

6 It's your son's second birthday. You've got a great idea:

a "Wouldn't it be brilliant to have all the children from nursery over for the day?"

b "Let's buy him a tricycle, with a metal rod so you can push from behind and take him for his first ride."

c "Couldn't we just keep quiet about it? He's only little, he'll never notice."

ANSWERS If you scored:

Mostly a To be **Super Dad** this far on means you're set for life, but you can't keep taking those drugs forever.

Mostly b **Fun Dad**, you're hanging on in there, learning, getting bruised, but doing a great job.

Mostly c You're not so much a **Slack Dad** as a man who is in denial. Lighten up – it can be fun!

Why your **toddler needs you**

She will test her boundaries constantly, want to do everything herself. Yet she will still seek you out as a person she really trusts, who really understands her needs. When she draws a picture of people who matter to her, you will be there. The only question is whether she draws you on the edge or right beside her.

Can you be solid, warm, gentle, and energetic?

You need to be a rock for him, something solid, always there, calm when he loses his cool. But the rock must also be warm and gentle, and find loads of energy to engage, appreciate, and enjoy your lives together. Impossible? Your toddler needs you because:

1 He wants to talk and talk. You understand his limited language and know what he's been up to, so you won't be mystified and ignore what he's saying.

2 She likes playing "Giant Feet" where she puts her tiny feet on yours and strides around shouting "Fee, Fi, Fo Fum".

3 When he gets tired walking, you pick him up. By the time he's three or four, he may be too heavy for your partner.

4 When she's screaming blue murder, kicking and shouting about not wanting a bath, you hold her, and walk calmly upstairs asking if she would like to put the bubbles in.

5 You've sung *Twinkle Twinkle Little Star* together a million times and know all the different ways he likes to change the song.

6 She loves finding ladybirds. And you can make the little plastic container with air holes in it, so she can catch and look at them.

7 You can hold him while he stands on the loo seat and does the highest wee ever.

8 When you're out in the street, even when you're talking to someone else, you never quite relax your vigilance, and catch her if she wanders into the road.

9 He hides under the bed covers for the fifth time, shouting, "Can't find meeee" and you're still amazed when he jumps out and reveals himself.

10 You keep serving her green vegetables, even though she says "yuck" every time. You don't make a fuss, because you know that, one day – God knows when – she'll start eating them.

TOY STORY

Police had to mount a search for a four-year-old boy who drove off in a toy truck from a shop in Northern Ireland. The boy disappeared from the shop behind the wheel of the "Step 2 Might Mac", the only such model in the store. Police said a van would have been needed to transport the toy out of the car park. Closed-circuit cameras recorded the child driving out of the front door with an adult couple hurrying behind on foot. The theft was only noticed when staff spotted the purple-and-yellow truck was missing a few hours later.

Separated dads

The first few years after the birth of a child is the danger time for relationships. Many break up, sometimes deeply acrimoniously. Being separated from your child, perhaps seeing little or nothing of him, is a devastating blow. If you find yourself without contact, seek a solution, first and foremost through conciliation and mediation with your child's mother. Treat the courts as a last resort. But, however hard it is to see him, never, ever give up on your child. Quietly slipping away, so there are no more conflicts, is not the answer. It might seem to be at the time, but your child will not forgive you.

RADICAL MUM

"My husband was violent to me, so I left with our son who was five. But Jack suffered greatly when we split up. He missed his dad. I didn't want to crush his father. I knew Jack was safe: his dad's anger had been towards me. So I've made sure that they see plenty of each other. To be honest, my ex does more with him now than before, when he was too busy. My message to Jack is that I still care for his dad and he should too. His dad deserves respect. I don't understand when separated fathers can see their children only every fortnight. I'd be devastated if I couldn't see Jack."
Sharon, mother of Jack

Looking after her

If you have the child only occasionally – at weekends or during holidays – research shows that she will settle best when, during visits, she is able to enjoy ordinary family activities like eating together, going for walks, or watching TV together. It isn't easy, especially if you've left the family home and you are short of money.

Keep in touch

Make sure that you are in touch with what's going at your child's nursery or school. If you have Parental Responsibility (*see p.42*), you are entitled to reports on your child's progress and access to health records.

p.42

Get support

If your child is very young – and you have not had much time caring for him alone – then look for support from grandparents and family. If your ex-partner knows that your child is being really well cared for when you have him, she will feel more confident in you and less likely to create barriers to contact.

Don't leave me

A ten year old recalls the time, four years earlier, when dad left:
"I can't remember the very day but I can remember a couple of weeks later when he came to visit me and I didn't know where he'd gone or anything. So he kept on visiting me and he kept on driving off in the car. I had this rocking horse by the window, and I used to sit up on the rocking horse and watch his car into the distance. I used to cry my eyes out all night and most of the day."

I miss dad

A young daughter talks about her Saturday Dad:
"I see dad every weekend. At first I thought I was never going to see him ever again…I just miss him quite a lot in the week now, but I don't feel like I'm never going to see him again and that I'm going to cry every night. I just miss him in the week. When I'm going on a visit, I get butterflies in my belly 'cos I'm so excited!"

He's still there

A princess discusses separation:
"When my dad told me, I was really sad because I've always been with my dad most of the time. But I can ring my dad whenever I like, I can see him and everything else. That's like before. He used to call me his princess star, and he named stars after me…"

A new family

An eight year old worries that second families can get in the way:
"I asked my dad if we were ever going to get pushed out, and he said never. He said he wouldn't do that in his whole entire life."

DAD TALK

"The stereotype of the weekend father as a sad, remote, emotionally inarticulate stranger passing a few hours with his kids in parks and burger restaurants may be accurate in a few cases, but it doesn't match my experience. Nor does the American idea of the "Disneyland Dad" – a man who ruins his kids with expensive treats. From the outset, I couldn't afford it. These days, the world of the weekend father is the world of homework, Playstations, frank conversation, and lazy Saturday mornings at home – not that of the frenetic entertainer or the tragicomic clown. It's just a different kind of normality."

Andrew Purvis, father of three

HOW TO BE GOOD PARENTS APART

Things may not have worked out for you as lovers, but you will always be parents together. Your children will do better if they see plenty of mum and dad and if the two of you get along.

- Don't use the kids to get at your partner.
- Be positive about your ex in front of the children.
- Be reliable – keep your promises to your children and to your ex.
- Avoid the courts if you possibly can. Bite your tongue, conciliate, and get mediation. Try everything you can before resorting to the courts – it will drive you further apart and cost a fortune.

Toddler **playtime**

Play is work for a toddler. You don't need toys, but, sometimes, it helps to start playing yourself, so he'll join in. Other times, let him get on with it by himself.

But how should I play?

I asked Mark Shepherd, a child minder and former home dad, who spent two years studying how to play with toddlers.

"You're trying to build their confidence. So it's important to let them do things without you getting too involved. But, sometimes, they don't know how to do it, so you start playing yourself, drawing, painting, building, and then they'll want to do it too. You don't ignore them, because they will be saying, 'Dad, look at what I've done.' But you have to listen carefully.

"I was at the bank the other day and a little boy was building with bricks. He called to his dad and said, 'Look at my rocket.' His dad looked and said, 'That doesn't look like a rocket'. Straight away, after his dad turned around, the boy smashed it up and ran off. His dad missed it but he had ruined his play. That child might think twice about building something with blocks and showing it to his dad again.

"For children, if they are pretending to cook, then it's work. So if they show you something they have done, say things like, 'You've spent a lot of time doing that.' They're not asking you whether it's good, because, in a child's eye, everything they do is good, it's the best they can do. If you jump in too quickly and say 'That's a wonderful picture of a car', when actually it's a ship, you're going to knock his confidence. He's going to think he's no good at drawing ships."

Start playing yourself, drawing, painting, building, and then they'll want to do it too

Five great games to play with your toddler

It's hard to choose when you've got finger painting, building blocks, jigsaws, balls, bats... but these ideas from Mark Shepherd (*see opposite*) are simple, cheap, and brilliant.

1 **Treasure baskets:** Fill a basket, bucket, or saucepan with household items such as spoons, sit your child between your legs, and he'll play happily for 30 minutes.

2 **Cups and stones:** All you need are a few plastic cups and some stones. One day a stone will be money, another day food, another day wall-building material. Suitable from six months to five years.

3 **Washing up:** Give her a few pots and pans to wash up. She'll get wet, your kitchen will get messy – but it's great fun.

4 **Paper mosaics:** Cut up bits of paper or card, preferably coloured, into 2cm (1in) squares. Then let him stick them together into patterns.

5 **Water cups:** Pouring water from one plastic cup into another will delight your toddler – and helps her develop hand-eye coordination.

Playing at home

Everything is play: getting dressed, eating, brushing teeth, opening the post, flushing the toilet, looking in the fridge. The challenge is making time to share in your child's experiences.

1 Let him help you do your chores. If you're sweeping, give him a little brush. If you're shaving, let him soap your face.

2 Play hide and seek, but don't find her too quickly – she'll try the same places again and again.

3 He is learning to scribble and draw. So let him try different types of felt pens and crayons.

4 Finger painting is brilliant. Cover a table with paper and let her paint all over it.

5 Dressing up games and pretend tea parties are always popular – just don't use your best china.

6 Get a mini chalkboard, a few pieces of chalk, and a duster. He'll play with them for hours.

7 Baking is fun. There's finding the ingredients, weighing, heating things, stirring, cutting out shapes, and eating the final product. Great!

8 Make cards for someone you haven't seen lately. Grandparents love to get one. Think glitter.

9 Pretend to post your child. Wrap her in pretend paper, stick pretend sticky tape on, write the address (tickly), stamp her, and post.

10 Have a treasure hunt. Leave notes all around the house with pictures on, telling him where to go next to find the treasure.

...and away

Going out can be so exciting even if it's just a walk to the shop, to post a letter, or to visit a neighbour around the corner.

1 Make a picnic. All you need is a few pieces of bread, fillings, fruit, and drinks. Let him help make and wrap up the sandwiches.

2 Tongue-holding competitions are useful when everyone gets out of hand in the car.

3 A ball and a bat are all you need in a green space. Start playing with them yourself and soon your child will want to join in, too.

4 Maybe it's time to get a dog. Children will go out in all weathers if the dog comes too.

5 Supermarket shopping can be a huge release for your child. Big, safe spaces to run and slide, trolleys to push – playtime.

6 Museums and galleries are excellent for rainy days. Not for the exhibits, though they may help, but for the free, open spaces.

7 There is no place quite like a playground for running, jumping, climbing, and meeting people. Great for both of you.

8 Go to church. It sounds strange, but toddlers love taking the collection, giving out the prayer books, and blowing out the candles.

9 Keep a kite at hand. They are thrilling for a child and modern ones are easy to use.

10 Taking him swimming gives you both a chance to let off steam and have fun.

Potty **training**

Children learn how to wee and poo in a potty or loo at different ages. It is counterproductive to rush them. So look out for the signs that they are ready to learn, help them, but be cool. They'll get there.

Natural development

Getting control of bladder and bowels is, like walking, part of a child's natural development – they don't need to be taught. But you can encourage them, usually from two to two and a half, though boys may not be ready until they are three.

When to start

You'll know if it's worth trying, because your child will say he's done something in his nappy, or may be dry after a nap. Produce the potty and leave it around for a few days. Next, pick a couple of weeks, perhaps in the summer,

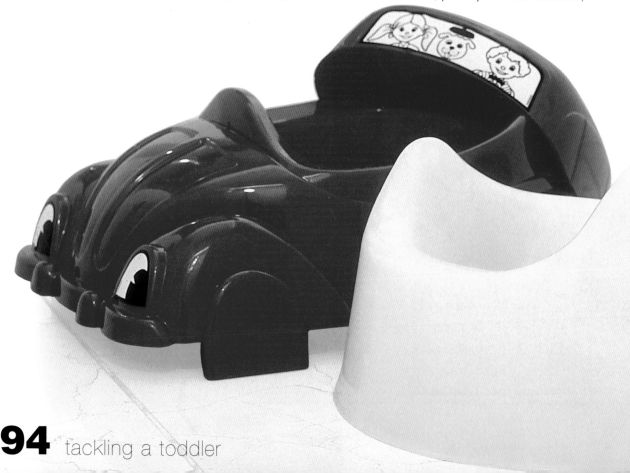

when you or your partner are usually at home with your child, put her in trainer pants or knickers. Times of change, such as moving house or a death in the family, are not good for potty training.

Give encouragement

Suggest that she sits on the potty after meals, at bath time, or after a sleep. Have a chat or play with a toy, so she sits for a while. Congratulate your child when she delivers and wipe her bottom (wipe a girl from front to back). If he has an accident, don't make a big deal. Lots of accidents mean he's not ready. Go back to nappies for a few weeks.

The next steps

If everything goes well, then keep your child in pants all day, putting her into trainer pants at night or for long journeys. But keep reminding her to use the loo, especially when she's tired. You can also put her on the loo with a clip-on child seat to help make sure she doesn't fall off. And children love flushing. Soon, she'll be waking you up at night to go to the loo.

HOME OFFICE TIP

If you work at home, always, if possible, have your office next to the loo. It is the place where your child will spend a great deal of time. He'll need help getting on and off, washing and drying hands, and so on. It gives you a quick break and keeps you in touch with his day. Overheard shouts of "Daddy, come and wipe my bottom", can only endear you to office-based clients and colleagues.

STAYING DRY AT NIGHT

Take your time before keeping him out of nappies overnight. But it's worth trying if his nappy is dry every morning for a week.

Let your child sleep with nothing on his bottom at night, not even pyjamas, on a protective bed sheet. If he wets the bed, he's not ready to go without nappies. You may find that months after being dry, a child starts wetting the bed, probably after some disruption or upset. Never scold or punish. Put him back in nappies for a while and then start the process all over again after a week of dry nappies.

Mapping out
the toddler years

Your child will surprise you daily: waking you up, probably far too early, with his latest curious discovery, desperate for you to play with him, responding to your love with great affection, expressed physically and verbally. At 12 months, he probably can't walk, but by four years old he's only months away from school days.

PHYSICAL

By two years, your toddler will probably:

- Know how to walk unsupported, stop, and be able to turn.

- Be able to run, but may fall over a lot.

- Climb safely into the car.

- Throw a ball and unscrew an item.

- Squat to pick something up and be able to stand up again.

And by three/four years...

- Pedal a tricycle and climb a small tree.

- Walk upstairs leading with either foot. Hop, skip, and jump.

- Push himself on a low swing unaided.

- Run fast without falling over much.

- Kick a ball confidently and stop it with her foot or with her hands.

- Turn over pages of a book, one at a time, and draw a circle on some paper.

DAD'S JOURNEY

In a few years, you go from pushing a buggy or carrying him in a sling to only occasionally carrying him on your shoulders on a long walk. From life being about changing nappies, it's about asking him if he needs to go to the loo. At bedtime, he used to coo at a simple picture, now at the age of four he may recognize individual letters like "G" is for gorilla. He wants

INTELLECTUAL

By two years, your toddler will probably:

- Enjoy pretend play, because her imagination has developed.

- Become possessive of certain things as "hers".

- Towards her second birthday, she starts to take an interest in potties – boys may take longer.

- Remember simple events that occur frequently and regularly.

- Enjoy looking at books with you and alone.

And by three/four years...

- Be able to sit on the loo for a wee or a poo.

- Speak in full sentences of four or five words.

- Be able to count to five.

- Sort objects by colour.

- Play hide-and-seek with you, hiding himself or going to find you when you hide.

- Be understood by people who don't know him well.

SOCIAL AND EMOTIONAL

By two years, your toddler will probably:

- Be happy about being apart from you and his mother for longer periods.

- Be very loving to a toy, pet, or another child.

- Be closely attached to you, his mother, and any siblings.

- Begin to think about how he feels and how others feel.

- Spot when you are not happy.

And by three/four years...

- Understand what her birthday is, anticipating it with pleasure.

- Be capable of a great range of emotions from sheer pleasure to frustrated rage.

- Be ready to stay in a nursery or with a child minder all day without either you or your partner.

- Express verbal affection to you and her mother.

- Have special friends of her own age of whom she is particularly fond.

to be independent and your challenge is to be patient enough and have time so that you can let him learn without taking over and stifling that great energy burning inside him. There are moments, increasingly lengthy, when he is occupied and playing well on his own, when you and your partner can catch up with each other.

Child-proof your home

Suddenly your home seems a dangerous place. Follow these tips and keep a first-aid box locked away with bandages, sterile gauze pads, plasters, scissors, tweezers, a thermometer, and a first-aid book.

1 Put away tablecloths – toddlers haven't mastered the trick of pulling them off and leaving the crockery in place.

2 Cover sharp edges and corners of furniture. Reinforce glass doors with anti-shatter, plastic film.

3 Cover electrical wall sockets and keep radiators and fireplaces out of reach. Set your water heater no higher than 48°C (120°F) to prevent burns.

4 Avoid using the front hobs on your cooker and do not leave hot food or drinks near table edges.

5 Your child's highchair can tip over. Stop other children from climbing on it and strap your child in.

6 Tie a knot in plastic bags, putting them out of reach. Likewise, remove deflated balloons and small objects that could choke a child.

7 Make sure your furniture is sturdy enough not to fall over if your child pulls herself up on it – especially check that drawers can't fall out.

8 Keep medicines, disinfectants, cleaning products, gardening products, paints, and beauty products out of reach of your child.

9 Cover or fence off any exposed water around your home. Never leave your toddler alone in the bath.

10 Check out your garden for poisonous plants and remove them or, for example, with laburnum, prevent it from flowering.

Choosing **child care**

At some point, you and your partner may decide that you should trust your child regularly with someone else – a child minder, play group, or nursery. Perhaps, it is so that both of you can work or because your child is getting older and needs more stimulation, contact with other children, and a more structured environment. You will want your child to be safe, happy, and thriving. There is plenty you can do to ensure a smooth transition, your own peace of mind, and top-class care for your child.

What's right for you?

The first step is to decide what type of child care is right for you and your child – and whether you can afford it. Is a nanny, child minder, or nursery the appropriate option? If you choose a nanny or child minder then you need to look for someone with a caring nature, who has had experience with children. The person does not necessarily need to have children of their own. The carer should be someone with an attitude to children similar to yours and your partner's, using a similar system of rewards and sanctions.

Hand-over time

It's a good idea to keep a note of your child's routine a few weeks before hand over, so the carer understands your child's typical

> Decide what type of child care is right for you and your child

day. With a nanny, you might need a week's hand-over time. With a child minder, it is good for you and your partner to spend time in the carer's home with your child, both to acclimatize the child and so you really feel confident that there is a good understanding between child and child minder. With a nanny, you could show her local parks or playgroups and introduce her to your local family friends and other nannies.

Choosing a nursery

If you decide on nursery care, check out if there is plenty of space – is there a garden where the children can play in dry weather? Ensure that there is a generous adult-to-child ratio. Ask them – and a child minder – for their most recent Ofsted report. They should offer it willingly or you can access it at www.ofsted.gov.uk. Seek personal recommendations on nurseries from friends. When you check one out, consider whether it is a calm, caring environment,

which is also stimulating. Are the children all busily engaged? Does each child have a key worker – the person they really identify as their carer? Before making a final choice, visit twice at different times of day.

Seek personal recommendations on nurseries from friends

Don't just speak to the manager – talk to helpers and speak to parents dropping off or picking up.

Settling in

Organize your work so that you allow some settling-in time – don't expect everything to go smoothly in the first few days. In particular, if this is your child's first time at nursery, expect her to be ill a lot in the first couple of months as she establishes immunity to children's infections.

MARK'S STORY

As a home dad, Mark Shepherd looked after other people's children on an ad hoc basis. "I received compliments from people saying, 'Mark, you're really good with them'. So I did a two-year course in Child Studies. You learn how to build their confidence and self-esteem and, most important, when to leave them to play.

"I was the first man in five years to do my course. I did 800 hours of placements – including one as a nanny for four weeks – which was tough because the placements caused us problems caring for our own daughter. But my managers' reports said I was obviously in the right job.

"Then I began my child-minding service starting with three under-fives. I was booked up without even advertising. People don't seem to mind me being a man. They say it's great to have a child in this environment. Now, I'm planning to open a nursery."

GETTING INVOLVED

Chances are, you probably left researching nurseries to your partner. Nevertheless, if you make the effort, you'll feel glad that you visited a couple of options, talked to staff, and took part in the choice. Drop your child off or pick him up regularly so you can tune into his life there and know the people who care for him. Nurseries would typically like more male presence and usually welcome dads staying for an hour or two, playing with the children. It helps your child become more confident, helps you to get to know his friends, and will give you good ideas on how to play with your child at home.

Toddler **masterchef**

The trick for ensuring that your toddler eats well is to establish a varied, nutritious diet. That won't be easy. Your child might refuse vegetables, for example, for years. But don't fuss. Keep presenting them even if they go uneaten, or "hide" them in casseroles or pasta dishes. Try to eat together as a family regularly, with everyone sharing a similar meal if possible.

Breakfast

Here are four suggested menus for a healthy toddler breakfast:

Fortified cereal with milk
Slices of fruit
Small glass of diluted fruit juice

Porridge
1 small banana
Small glass of warm milk

Wholemeal toast with jam
Pot of yoghurt or fromage frais
Slices of fruit
Small glass of diluted fruit juice

Boiled egg with toast soldiers
Slices of fruit
Pot of yoghurt or fromage frais
Small glass of warm milk

Lunch and dinner

Find recipes that you can enjoy as a family. Here are some suggestions:

Raw vegetables with
hummus dip
Turkey stir-fry with noodles
Fruit smoothie
Small glass of water or milk

Chicken, rice, and peas
Slices of fruit
Glass of water

Spaghetti bolognese
Green salad
Small glass of diluted fruit juice

Small baked potato with tuna
Custard with banana slices
Small glass of diluted fruit juice

BREAKFAST TIP

In the morning, a glass of warm milk, or milk substitute, can be a popular part of breakfast. But it's worth holding this back until your toddler has eaten his cereal, toast, or fruit first so that he doesn't fill up on the milky drink instead and refuse to eat.

GINGERBREAD MEN

These are easy to make and fun to cut out, decorate, and give as presents, especially after reading the story about the couple who bake themselves a gingerbread boy. The boy shouts "Let me out", bursts from the oven, and escapes, pursued by various animals, until finally being eaten by a sly fox. Make sure you handle the hot stuff.

You need:

> 115g sugar
> 280g plain flour
> 1 tsp ground ginger
> ½ tsp of bicarbonate
>   of soda
> 115g margarine
> 3 tbsps golden syrup
> White icing sugar
> Biscuit cutters

Oven Temperature: 180°C (350°F)
Cooking Time: 15 minutes

Method:

- Your child helps to weigh out the sugar and puts it in a saucepan. Next, he weighs the flour and sifts it into a bowl with the ginger and bicarbonate of soda. He weighs the margarine and adds it, with the golden syrup, to the saucepan – he will love to lick the spoon.

- Stir the contents of the saucepan on the hob until it is warm and pour the mixture into a mixing bowl. Add the flour, ginger, and bicarbonate of soda. Your toddler can then help mix it until it is stiff.

- Ask your child to sprinkle some flour on the table, tip your mixture onto it, and you can both have a turn rolling it out thinly. He will love to cut out the gingerbread-men shapes. (You can adapt this recipe, using different cutters to make angels, Santas, and snowmen for Christmas, or bunnies at Easter.)

- Place the shapes on a baking tray covered in non-stick paper and put them in the oven until they start to brown. Be careful not to overcook – children like them best when they are soft on the inside.

- When you think the biscuits are ready, get your toddler to shout, like the gingerbread boy in the tale, "Let me out, let me out."

- Cool the biscuits on a wire tray for 5–10 minutes. Now your child can decorate the biscuits with icing (mix together icing sugar and a drop of water), glacé cherries, raisins, or anything you have to hand.

Dealing with **tantrums**

Your child is gaining a sense of self and wants to be independent. But life is frustrating because she either can't or is not allowed to do everything that she wants. There are also many hazards to upset a toddler – the insecurity, for example, of being separated from you or your partner. Tiredness, boredom, hunger, thirst, and the final stages of teething are all issues that can

If your child thinks tantrums succeed in him getting his own way then you are going to see a lot more of them

send your young child into a spin. Although she may be walking, she is likely to be unsteady at times – life is a series of accidents, falls, and injuries. Any of these factors can lie behind a tantrum – kicking and screaming, hitting out at other children, refusing to cooperate, even holding his breath until he turns blue in the face. It can be very upsetting and a big test for you.

Understanding why

It is vital to stay calm and understand the reasons why your child has lost self-control. It will help you anticipate her needs, perhaps for more time with you, for more interesting things to do, or simply for more regular drinks and snacks.

Stay in control

If all hell breaks loose with a tantrum, there are a few things you can do. Do not appease a tantrum. That can be hard if, for example, he is shouting, screaming, and flinging himself about in the supermarket, but try not to worry too much about what other people are thinking. Focus instead on the fact that, if your child thinks tantrums succeed in him getting his own way, then you are going to see a lot more of them.

The naughty corner

You will need time and patience. If you have neither, your child will take advantage of you. Have a place for time out – a "naughty corner" – because you cannot reason with him until he has calmed down. Tell him why he is there. Don't hit him. Do not shout at him, but lower your voice so he knows you are cross with him. Don't take it personally. This is a healthy part of your child's development. Leave him for a few minutes and then come back. If he will not stay, then sit down with him and keep him there. Be kind but firm.

Praise good behaviour

Don't change your mind and do not reward bad behaviour. As soon as your child begins to behave well again, praise her and encourage her.

AGONY UNCLE

Q: What should I do if I've had a tantrum and lost my temper with my child?

A: Don't be afraid to apologize – you might find it hard to do so, but you will always be glad when you do it, if you have shouted or been unfair. It is good for children to know that their mum and dad sometimes get things wrong as well.

GOOD DISTRACTIONS

Maintain routines and avoid potential confrontations. But when your toddler is about to explode into a temper tantrum, try some good distractions – they really do work.

- If he won't put on his coat, find a toy to play with, and slip the coat on as you are playing.

- Help your child to feel she has choices. If she always says "no" to the clothes you suggest, pick out two shirts and let her decide which one to wear.

- When he is stubborn, make a joke such as: "If you don't put on your shoes, I'll have to tickle you."

- If your child is banging the TV, offer her a biscuit tin and tell her it makes a much louder noise.

- Make difficult issues into a game: at bedtime, compete to see who can get into bed first. He'll want to win.

DAD TALK

"Love the children enough to say or do the wrong things, to stumble together, to expose one's frailty."

Rowan Williams, father of two, and Archbishop or Canterbury

Step**fathering**

A stepfather has to be an amazing man, someone expected to take on a role that is essential, yet ill-defined, with children whose births and first years he may have missed. He may be the object of anger from the children and their biological dad. Yet those children may also really need a stable, male figure in their lives. It's a tough act in a culture that rarely appreciates a stepdad's virtues.

How to avoid the pitfalls

Originally, a stepfather "stepped" into the role of a dead father. Today, that's all changed – there is usually another father, the biological dad. You can't replace him. But, if you avoid the pitfalls, there's a great opportunity to share in your stepchildren's lives.

1 Be patient if your stepchildren are not as delighted about your relationship with their mother as you are. They probably wish their parents had not split up.

2 If you are not already a parent, why not go on a parenting course and learn as much as possible?

3 Don't become the authority figure. You may be pressurized to be by your partner, but the kids will hate it. Support her, instead, to discipline them.

4 Encourage the establishment of clear household rules for tricky areas, like tidying up and bedtimes.

5 You should not feel guilty if you do not love your stepchildren – or you feel more for your biological children. But be fair and loving towards them.

6 Avoid conflict over money. Say what you can contribute and what the biological father should pay for – school trips, new clothes, treats, etc.

7 Don't expect the kids to call you "Dad". They will find a name for you; be content with whatever it is.

8 If your stepchildren push you away, do not assume that it is because you are a stepfather. It may simply be part of their development.

9 Avoid falling out with your stepchildren's biological father. You aren't competing for the children, even if you were for their mother.

10 If your relationship breaks down, try to stay in your stepchildren's lives – they may have already have lost one father.

Having **another child**

Your partner may barely have stopped breastfeeding the baby when virtually every passing stranger starts asking about the next one. Don't get pushed into a decision. If you do want another, some say that a small age gap means the children are more likely to be friends. Others think that a bigger gap means that you have more energy for each child. A big issue, especially for a dad.

Preparing for the arrival

The birth of a second child can be a difficult time – many break-ups occur at this stage. But it offers opportunities for dads. "We gave our second child a womb name, 'Bubbles'," says Michael. "As he grew, we chatted with his sister about what it would be like to have a baby brother. It helped her prepare for the arrival of 'her' baby. She realized it would be a mixed blessing – new babies were fun, but also annoying."

A new brother

As the birth came closer, Michael's four year old needed him. "Taking her to her various activities fell to me, as did bedtime and early mornings. At weekends we were increasingly on our own at the swimming pool, in the park, and cooking in the kitchen. The old threesome became more of a twosome." And then came the birth. "Our daughter needed assurance about what was happening and I phoned her frequently during the labour. When her brother arrived she was top of the call list and the first into the hospital to see the new baby."

After the birth

A dad's job supporting a sibling doesn't finish with the birth. "In the evenings," Michael explains, "my partner had to focus on feeding and bathing the new baby. It was important for me to be there for our older child – bathing her, preparing her for bed, reading her stories, and giving her plenty of attention."

AGONY UNCLE

Q What goes through a child's mind when his parents have another baby?

A: Dr Sebastian Kraemer, an internationally respected consultant child psychiatrist, explains: "An older child will usually feel tremendous affection for the new arrival, but he may also be annoyed to discover what his parents have done. When there are just two parents, then the child feels that two's company, but he is quickly shocked to discover that three is a crowd. Nevertheless, a sibling relationship can be a very important preparation for a child. It helps him prepare for adult relationships. A child has to learn to stick at it, to fight and then make up, because you can't get divorced."

HOW TO SUPPORT SIBLINGS

Chat with your child about the baby. Let him talk about how he might be missing mummy or how he might be fed up with the baby for taking all her time. You can even admit that you miss mum as well so that your child feels understood. If you have a younger sibling, talk about what the baby's arrival was like for you. Include your older child in as many of the preparations as possible. He can help blow up the balloons and make the "Welcome Home" banner for when mother and baby return. There are also some excellent children's books to share on the issue, notably *Good Girl Gracie* by Hilda Offen (Gareth Stevens) and *Sophie and the New Baby* by Laurence and Catherine Anholt (Albert Whitman & Co).

school
days

Will they be the best days of her life? Have you picked a good one? Suddenly, she's in a school uniform, **away from home all day**, an angel in the Christmas play. He's learning his spellings, **sounding out his letters**, struggling with his sums, **naming dinosaurs**. There's homework, tests, Brownies and Cubs, sleepovers, fall-outs with friends, **a place in the football team**. There are screeching violins, noisy playgrounds, **no more kisses goodbye at the gate**. Halfway to 18, she seems to have only just started and yet, already, you begin to wonder: **"Where next?"**.

Choosing a **primary school**

Finding a school for your child can be stressful. You or your partner may not have fond memories of education, or you might have lost touch with what makes a "good" school. You may fear that your lack of preparation will forever damage your child's chances of success, and feel wrong-footed by other parents who seem to have been organized since their children were embryos. Don't panic. You will find a good school.

When to apply

Children are legally required to be in full-time education by the term of their fifth birthday. Your local education authority will contact you in the preceding year about how to apply. If you don't hear from them, begin to make enquiries yourself.

Where are the schools?

The first step is to identify the schools in your area for which your child is eligible. Catchment areas can vary annually, depending on birth rates and popular demand, so you will need to speak to each school about their admission criteria – for example, religious schools may have a preference for church goers. Also, each education authority operates slightly differently.

OFSTED reports

Building up a picture of a school involves piecing together a jigsaw. The school's latest Ofsted report is a good start. It will tell you quite a bit about the school – class sizes, its social make-up, its ethos, its areas of success, its expertise, which may, for example, lie in special needs, literacy, or creative arts. Alarm bells should ring if it was judged "unsatisfactory", but "satisfactory" means the school is fine. Look out for value-added details – such as how much a school has succeeded in moving a child on academically, from entrance to leaving. League tables based on examination results (taken at age 10 or 11) are useful, but should not be used in isolation.

Can I make a visit?

Once you have selected a school you are interested in, speak to the headteacher to arrange a visit. See how engaged the children are in the tasks they are doing, and how polite and happy they are. How big is the playground or outdoor play area? How good are the PE facilities and the computer suites? Are there interactive white boards? It is also important to speak to parents with children at the school, if you can.

Going private

Knowledge is power. This applies to an even greater degree if you are considering private education. Private schools – known as pre-prep schools – start early (at age 4). They are inspected, but not by Ofsted, so it is even more important that you take the initiative and do your homework.

BEING A GOVERNOR

One third of school governors must be parents and typically at least some of the posts come up for election each year. Parent govenors bring vital expertise in finance, building development and maintenance, educational issues, and dealing with local government. Governors are powerful – they appoint the head teacher, are responsible for the budget, and decide spending priorities.

You can also join the school's parent-teacher association (PTA), which helps raise money, offers you a chance to meet other parents, and gives you an understanding of how well the school is working.

A father's place is
in the classroom

Even if most primary teachers are women and most parents at the gate are mums, the research is clear: your role at school is crucial.

Gareth Todd-Jones, a head teacher in Wales, took dads out for a pint and set up a local activity group for fathers and their children. "People here have a rough, tough image of what it is to be a man," he says. "They thought they weren't meant to do anything with their children. But now our dads go camping with the kids, cook, make cards for Mothers' Day, do woodwork, sew, and make weaving frames."

Robert Davies, father of three, adds: "Most men like me didn't know how to interact with their children before this group came along. I am now closer than ever to my children. Their behaviour is unrecognizable. It's amazing that just me being involved in their lessons makes them think of school as fun. They're ahead in all their classes."

What's in it for your child?

Your involvement in your child's learning is associated with a host of good outcomes. Typically, your child will have better-quality interpersonal relationships, good mental health, better exam results, better school attendance, and he is less likely to get involved in crime. That's official. You can really make a difference – so don't hang back, get involved.

Help out – volunteer for school trips

It's all about being there

Even if your child's school does not actively encourage parents to be involved, you can quietly and diplomatically be there for your child. When you drop her off, or pick her up, arrive a bit early, so that you have time to visit her classroom and she can proudly show you her latest piece of work, a drawing, or some writing.

Look ahead

Make sure you read the school newsletter every week, so you know what's coming up. When is his class performing at assembly? You may have to go to work an hour later, but he will love you coming to watch. Keep an eye on what the class topic is for the term. Does it involve anything in which you have special knowledge? You could ask the teacher if she wants you to come in for an hour to speak to the class. Teachers often ask for parent volunteers for school trips – it's worth sacrificing a day's holiday once a year to help out. Then there are after-school clubs – computing, craft, cooking, or sports. Could you make time occasionally to help out?

Help out at home

At home, there is also a lot you can do. Read with your child, help with her homework, do spelling tests, or help her with Internet research for school topics. Learn something with her – perhaps a musical instrument.

Quick quiz:
do you know each other?

Photocopy this page so that you and your child can do the quiz at the same time. Dad and child fill in both answers to each question. So, for example, your child writes down both her best friends and who she thinks are your best friends. Then compare each other's answers. Hopefully, you'll have a laugh, discovering what you did not know about each other. No cheating!

1 Name your two best friends:

CHILD

....

....

DAD

....

2 What is your favourite band or singer?

CHILD

....

DAD

....

3 What most frightens you?

CHILD

....

DAD

....

4 Name your favourite TV programme:

CHILD

....

DAD

....

5 If you could pick one dish when eating out what would it be?

CHILD

....

DAD

....

6 If you were feeling down, what would you really like someone to do for you?

CHILD

....

DAD

....

7 Which family trip have you most enjoyed?

CHILD

....

DAD

....

8 What is the phrase you use the most?

CHILD

....

DAD

....

9 What's the most exciting thing you've ever done?

CHILD

....

DAD

....

10 If you were an animal, which animal would you be?

CHILD

....

DAD

....

SCORES

Each person can get a maximum of 10 answers right. Give yourselves two marks for a right answer, one for a half-right answer. Add up both your scores into one number:

20–40 You two really know each other well. Reward yourselves with a trip to your child's favourite local place and a pint in dad's favourite pub.

10–20 You're pretty smart about each other's tastes, but you could do with a refresher course. How about a picnic together in your favourite park?

0–10 Oh dear, oh dear. Sounds like you need to go away together for a weekend. How about camping, a theme park, or a trip to see the grandparents?

Providing **life skills**

It's easy to forget how many life skills a dad helps his child to acquire. We're not just talking about teaching your son how to order a pint or put out the bins, or about showing him how to go to the toilet standing up. And setting your daughter on the road to life is more than helping her to understand what men do daily with a shaving brush and razor.

Like father, like son – or daughter

Your son will model himself on you. If you see other men as friends, so will he. And your relationship with your daughter is vital for her long-term relationships with men. Set a positive example for your child in all things, starting with being a good mentor and teaching the following life skills.

1. Looking after yourself. Take your child with you when you have your hair cut, or when you're buying yourself new clothes. He'll see you looking after yourself and follow suit.

2. Eating out. Learning to behave while eating in public is an important skill, so if there's spare cash, take your child to a restaurant and show her how it's done.

3. Making friends. Your child will spend lots of time with kids at nursery and school, but if you invite them home, those friendships can really blossom.

4. Riding a bicycle. Expect a bad back from running behind holding the seat, while your child learns to balance.

5. Swimming. Weekend mornings in the pool together are great fun – even if you never have a proper swim and freeze because you must dry your child first.

6. Painting, decorating, and DIY. They will be ready to pitch in with a paintbrush from the age of two. Involve them as they grow up and they will be confident DIYers for life.

7. Pets. Having a pet helps kids to respect and care for living things. Your job is to pay for it, clean it, and take it for walks.

8. Gardening. Watching a plant grow will fascinate your child. Even if you don't have your own garden, there's no reason why you can't share growing tomatoes in a tub outside your front door.

9. Cleaning. Tidy his room together. He'll join in and will own the final result. It might mean fewer rows come the teenage years.

10. Playing football. Knowledge and competence in soccer is vital for every boy – and most girls. Enrol your child in a club.

AGONY UNCLE

Q: I was always good at sport and want my child to do well, too. How should I encourage him?

A: Being a loving dad watching your kid playing sport can bring out the best and the worst in you. Sport gives kids obvious benefits of exercise, friendships, and, if channelled correctly, a competitive spirit. It is also a great father-and-child "bonder". But, go on, admit it, as dads we make every tackle, put away every volley, and break the tape with our children. We also share those after-match highs and lows.

Amid the emotion, it is sometimes difficult to avoid criticism. You can forget that your job is to be there for your child, no matter what. Win, lose, or draw, what's important is that your child gets something out of sport and is not just trying to please you.

Mapping out
the school years

Huge differences develop between children. At seven or eight, some can perform the intellectual tasks expected of an 11 year old. Children develop at their own pace, often in spurts. Many factors are involved, such as intelligence, health, emotional well-being, and ability to concentrate, but your support is crucially important.

PHYSICAL

By age 7, your child will probably:

- Be ready to learn to ride a bicycle without stabilizers.
- Be able to swim a width of a swimming pool.
- Be able to use scissors confidently.
- Be able to brush his teeth thoroughly himself.
- Be growing out of some childhood ailments such as asthma and allergies – though this is not true for all children.

And by 11...

- Need at least nine hours sleep at night.
- Show the first signs of puberty – breast development and pubic hair for a girl. Boys typically start around the age of 12.
- Be about to go through a big growth spurt over the next couple of years.

DAD'S JOURNEY

You have turned into a taxi driver, taking children to football practices, swimming lessons, gym classes, and seemingly weekly birthday parties. You are seeing less of your child because she has such a busy life and is tired by the time she gets home. The challenge for you is not to lose touch. The answer, particularly as she approaches adolescence, is to develop hobbies

INTELLECTUAL

By age 7, your child will probably:

- Be able to add and take away, write simple sentences, understand simple text, spell basic vocabulary, and use full stops and capital letters.

- Start moving from concrete thinking to more abstract thought.

- Want some detail on where babies come from.

- Know swear words. The best way to make clear bad language is wrong is not to use it yourself.

And by 11...

- Read fluently from a variety of fiction and non-fiction books.

- Write extended pieces in joined-up handwriting with correct punctuation and accurate spelling.

- Add, subtract, multiply, and divide.

- Measure distances, count money, tell the time, sort data, classify animals into groups, and speak in front of the class.

SOCIAL AND EMOTIONAL

By age 7, your child will probably:

- Be ready for a couple of after-school activities such as gym, learning a musical instrument, or Brownies and Cubs.

- Feel ready for a night away on a "sleep-over".

- Be ready to do a short trip with a friend to a nearby shop, provided there are no very busy roads to cross.

- Not feel separation anxiety when going to school, unless there is a problem there.

- Be less interested in playing with the opposite sex.

And by 11...

- Be ready to walk home from school with a friend, provided it is nearby and you have walked the route together in advance.

- Be accustomed to make decisions for herself.

- Get interested in the opposite sex again.

- Show the first signs of mood swings that can accompany adolescence.

that you share so you can do them together. It's probably the only way to make sure that you are in touch with her when she's always busy with her friends and when she turns into a door-slammer, saying, "Daaad, you are just so embarrassing". But remember, even the fastest-growing child will still enjoy a good story at bedtime.

Party planner

If you have a party at home, expect it to be trashed. And if you're planning to entertain without help, expect to be exhausted. Hiring a venue or an entertainer (or both) saves you effort, but can be costly. Set a budget, and talk to your child about what she wants.

Home or away?

Wherever you choose to hold the party, it should be a reasonably contained environment allowing space for food preparation, a play area, and sufficient toilet facilities. Wherever you are and whatever you are doing, you should be able to keep an eye on all of the children. Can your home cope? Set aside at least two hours for the party, including 45 minutes for eating.

Who's invited?

Send invitations out at least a couple of weeks in advance. A clash of events, leading to apologies, could really disappoint your child. Rule of thumb is that your child's age should roughly correspond with the number of guests. Certainly, start small with toddlers, but, by school age, the need to return invitations may transform the party into a whole-class extravaganza.

Preparation, preparation

Organize everything a few days beforehand (you can buy a lot of the paper goods by mail order). Ensure you have enough cups, plates, and napkins. Buy small toys in bulk from supermarkets to put in the home-time party bags. Games also need to be prepared in advance. Recruit a few adult helpers.

Simple fare

Keep food simple. Check dietary needs and cover a few basic tastes so every child likes something. Keep water and juice available so children can serve themselves. Avoid pre-meal nibbles that can distract from the games and spoil appetites.

The aftermath

Have plenty of bin bags ready for the clear up. They are also useful for carrying the presents (keep a list of who gave what). When the party's over, pour yourself a large gin.

BAKE A BIRTHDAY CAKE

If you want to impress all the parents – and your child – why not bake the birthday cake yourself? It's as easy as pie:

Ingredients:

175g caster sugar, 3 eggs,
50g butter, 2 x tbsps water, ½ tsp
vanilla essence, 125g plain flour,
3 x tbsps jam, icing sugar to sprinkle

oven temp: 190°C (375°F)
cooking time: 20–25 minutes

Method:

- Grease and line two
  18cm cake tins.
- Whisk the sugar and eggs
  for about 10 minutes.
- Heat the butter and water in a
  pan until the butter melts, and
  then pour into the whisked
  mixture. Add the vanilla essence
  and whisk for 30 seconds.
- Sieve in the flour and fold in.
- Bake for 20–25 minutes or
  until risen. Leave to cool, turn
  out, and sandwich together
  with the jam. Sprinkle the top
  with icing sugar to finish and
  stick in a candle – or 12!

DOUGIE'S STORY

Ex-RAF fighter pilot, Dougie Roxburgh, recently single-handedly organized a birthday party at the local village hall for his daughter, Francesca, 8, because his wife was away dealing with a family illness. He recalls: "I prepared the hall early, as setting the scene takes time. The balloons and streamers helped to create the atmosphere. I laid the table beforehand with the food ready to serve so I wasn't distracted by these tasks during the party.

"I know that kids like party rituals and organized games, like pass-the-parcel, so I had half a dozen ready. I made sure the games were inclusive so that all the children were participating for most of the time. I didn't want non-participants getting bored and wandering off. I had all the games ready to start in an instant. You have to be a master of ceremonies with a strong directing hand – otherwise anarchy can prevail."

Dosh for the kids ... but don't let them bankrupt you

Children get interested in money very early on. A trip to the bank can involve your toddler leaning across the counter to request "chocolate pennies" from the teller. But how much of the real stuff should your child have – and when?

Money wise

It's good for children to get familiar with money. When you go shopping, why not let your child pay and collect the change? It makes him feel more grown up, though it can be a struggle separating him from the change. In the supermarket, you could ask your child to check out how much everything costs as you pile up the trolley. He will begin

Pocket money will give her a sense of her own power and independence

to get a sense of relative value. It's good for his maths, too, comparing how much of one thing he could buy for so many of another. In no time, he can become quite good at guessing how much things cost. As he gets older, he may even ask how much you get paid at work and begin to consider how long you have to work to pay for something like a car or a bicycle.

Easy come, easy go?

Pretty soon, your child will have money of her own. Even if you don't give it to her, she can accumulate considerable sums from grandparents and birthday gifts. Pocket money, paid to your child each week, is important, especially if it is linked to doing particular tasks, such as keeping her clothes tidy, making her bed daily, or brushing her teeth. It will give her a sense of her own power and independence that she can go out and buy what she wants with her own money. But it will also start to teach her that money doesn't grow on trees – that she, just like her parents, has to do something useful and productive to earn it.

IS DAD A WALKING WALLET?

You may think that most children see their dads as walking wallets, there chiefly to earn the cash to pay for their mobiles and trainers. Wrong. In a survey of 230 British children, aged between 9 and 11, 64 per cent said that dad's most important job was looking after them, while just 22 per cent said it was going out to work.

The survey found the next generation of parents even more ambitious about the caring role of dads in the future. Nine out of ten girls said they would prefer the fathers of their children to be caring rather than rich. More than three quarters of the children believed it was OK for dad to stay at home looking after the children while mum went out to work. Perhaps most surprisingly, 72 per cent of boys agreed with the proposition.

DON'T GO BROKE

Children do need consumer goods, not least because they don't want to stand out from their peers. So if their friends have the latest designer clothes, trainers, or sports gear, it is hard to deny them the same. But sometimes you must say "no". You have to be brave and explain to your child that although she might miss out on the latest must-haves, this doesn't mean that she is inferior to her peers. Show her that style is about confidence and being an individual.

Letting them out **on their own**

It's a big world out there and it can be scary to think about letting your children venture into it alone. But you must give them independence to help them stay safe in the future.

Stranger danger

From an early age, you should drum into your child procedures to avoid "stranger danger". She should know never to speak to strangers. If she finds herself in an emergency, she should know to seek help from someone in a uniform, an official, or a shop assistant. If she is out with a group, say, at the zoo, she should never wander off on her own. Teach her your home telephone number as early as you can. Turn it into a song, so it is easier to remember.

She should know never to speak to strangers

Road safety

Teaching your child the basics of road safety – the Green Cross Code (*see panel opposite*) – is crucial if you are to feel confident about him crossing the road successfully on his own. Some schools teach road safety – it's worth finding out exactly what they teach, so you can reinforce the same message.

Look ahead

As your child heads towards 10 or 11 years of age, you should start thinking more about letting her go out on her own. It is difficult, especially with a first child, because the newspapers are so full of horror stories about what can happen to children. But if you don't start letting go, then the teenage years will come as a shock to you, as your child will want to make her own way to school and go out with her friends, unescorted by mum or dad.

Small steps

A first step towards letting your child out without you can be finding children nearby, of similar age, who you feel can be responsible friends to accompany your child. Talk to the children's parents and arrange what ground rules you will set for letting the children out together. You could start with the children being allowed to walk together from one home to the other. You can gradually build on this as their (and your) confidence grows.

On your bike

Some schools teach cycling proficiency, the basics of the Highway Code, and will actually give children lessons on the road. However, it will be down to you to help your child to ride a bicycle in the first place. Kit her out correctly, with a well-fitting helmet, from day one. Some children can manage without stabilizers as early as four or five years of age. You should take the time to make sure that your child can cycle unsupported by the age of eight. One brilliant way to ensure that your child is safe on a bicycle is to cycle with her – perhaps to school – on the road, with you initially on the outside, closer to the traffic, and her on the inside. Cycling together can be the start of a lifelong hobby that the two of you – and the rest of the family – can enjoy together. If she's a bit slow at first, perhaps you can get your running shoes out and jog alongside her while she is gaining confidence. You will become fitter and it will not be long before you aren't able to keep up with her.

> Cycling together can be the start of a lifelong hobby

Skateboarding

Your child may also want to know about how to skateboard and rollerblade. This could be an activity for both of you to learn together. Make sure you are both wearing the correct safety gear, including a helmet and protective clothing, and ensure that your child understands the importance of respect for other pavement users.

USING PUBLIC TRANSPORT

Anyone who has commuted at all has probably learned to hate public transport. But, to young children, even the shortest, most mundane trip on a bus or a train is fun. So leave the car at home and go by bus with your child whenever you can. If you stay relaxed and calm, it will help him to feel comfortable and at ease. Make sure he also understands when to pay and how to get on and off. These are really useful skills to learn early, and it will not be long before he is putting them to use by himself.

Disability and special needs

Up to one in five children, at some point in their lives, has a special educational need. Many difficulties can be dealt with successfully if identified early, so be ready to make a fuss, if necessary.

Possible problems

Children's difficulties can range from severe physical or mental impairment to more common issues such as ADHD, or attention deficit hyperactivity disorder (characterized by extreme restlessness and poor concentration), dyslexia (difficulty ordering letters), dyspraxia (poor coordination), and autism (including Asperger's syndrome). Some of these conditions require medical diagnosis and medication, but most require action by schools in partnership with parents in order to support the child.

Your child needs you to be smart – and a supporter not a critic

Severe disabilities

If your child has a physical disability that restricts movement, you need to make sure that his school is equipped to accommodate him. If he is in a wheelchair, liaise with the school to ensure that he can get around easily and is not excluded from activities, such as sports, if he would like to participate. A child with serious mental impairment needs schooling tailored to his specific requirements. Seek medical advice and work closely with the school to ensure your child benefits fully.

ADHD

A child with ADHD finds it difficult to concentrate, is constantly on the move, and has poor school performance compared with intelligence. Her behaviour is disruptive and she may have low self-esteem. ADHD is thought to affect 3–5 per cent of the school-age population and is estimated to be 3–4 times more common in boys. For some, there is remission at puberty but, untreated, the condition can continue in adulthood. There are effective drug treatments for ADHD and help from schools includes teaching in a series of short tasks, developing social skills, and using "time out" sessions to help children to calm down.

Dyslexia

Often related to the less common dyspraxia, dyslexia is a complex neurological disorder, affecting about 10 per cent of the population across all levels of intellectual ability. There are lots of manifestations beyond poor spelling, such as problems following oral instructions, and a poor sense of timing and direction. If you don't understand the problem, then you may easily criticize your child for something that is a fundamental part of her make-up. That's why a dyslexic child often suffers low self-esteem. More than most, this child needs you to be smart, and a supporter not a critic.

AUTISM: A FATHER'S STORY

Andy's son, Chris, was diagnosed with autism at the age of three and a half: "Chris had had several chest infections. At 15 months he went into hospital and came home a changed child, totally wrapped up in his own world. He didn't recognize what was happening around him, had lost his communication skills, and had no sense of danger. At three and a half he was diagnosed as autistic. "We had to teach him everything step by step – how to express his needs through gestures and symbols. We had to fight for schooling, transport, everything. A lot revolves around family centres, but most dads don't want it – it's the stigma. So I created my own support group for dads with disabled children. We meet in a pub twice a month. We go bowling, play pool – we can talk rather than sit and listen. Some men want to be out when their child is at home because of the behavioural problems; there are couples in trouble – we share strategies. Dads come for a while and then you might not see them for months. But they know we are here".

Making the most of **computers**

Reading a book fires the imagination, watching TV stimulates a child visually. But playing on a computer allows him to respond and make things happen. Like a lot of technology, the computer is a great device that dads can use with their children for learning and having fun. Play it safe and reap the benefits.

GREAT WEBSITES FOR KIDS

- www.bbc.co.uk/cbbc
- www.bbc.co.uk/schools
- www.build-it-yourself.com
- www.enchantedlearning. com
- www.factmonster.com
- www.funbrain.com
- www.gameskidsplay.net
- www.kidlink.org
- kids.msfc.nasa.gov
- www.ukchildrensbooks. co.uk
- www.yahooligans.yahoo. com

A good learning tool

Computers have a huge educational value – there are great programmes you can buy. It's vital that your child gains access to a vast source of knowledge. So go online together and show her how to find things that interest her and how to interact in a safe and responsible way. Kids learn really fast on computers and it can be something you share as she hands her expertise on to you.

Interactive websites

Trawl the computer for enjoyable interactive websites on which your child can learn and develop his skills (*see panel left*). You could seek advice from your child's school and tie in computer activities to the curriculum. Quizzes, puzzles, drawing activities, and computer games are all rewarding and educational. Set your child on his way and then let him continue.

The possible dangers

As with road safety, you can't always keep your child away from danger. You must explain the hazards and then let him get on with his life. The dangers of chat rooms are well documented – you don't always know who your child is talking to – though the rise in webcams should help. There is also a vast amount of pornography and violent imagery on the Internet that your child may access in error.

Firewall your kids

Make sure the computer is not a place for secrets. Keep it in a main room in the house, not in a bedroom, so that you can monitor what's going on. Make sure you have a parental control programme that filters out as much rubbish as possible and tutor your child against giving out any personal details, such as telephone numbers or address, online.

"We love going online together. Cole is mostly interested in checking out the children's programmes on the BBC site, looking up his favourite characters. We look at stories, play games, do colouring programmes. It's more interactive than a bedtime story. He thinks it's wonderful."
Tom, father of Cole age 5

Reading together

An upside of fatherhood is that, even though you haven't time to read Proust and Joyce, you can enjoy some great authors of our time – with your kids – because this is a golden age of children's literature.

Sharing stories

Mark Haddon's *The Curious Incident of the Dog in the Night-Time* is just one example of a book for children that adults have bought recently in vast quantities. The same is true of Harry Potter's adventures and *His Dark Materials* by Philip Pullman. Of course, adults have always enjoyed children's books – just think of "Winnie the Pooh" by AA Milne, published in the late 1920s. But there has never been quite the depth of appeal for adults in children's literature as there is today.

Serial pleasures

In short, it is a pleasure to read to your children, if you choose wisely and find books that will excite you as well. You'll find yourself battling with your partner to read to the kids at night, and waiting in suspense for the next chapter.

Reading solo

At some point – it may be as early as age five or six or much later, age eight or even nine – your child will begin to get interested in reading to himself. When that moment comes, all the time you put in encouraging him will feel well worthwhile. But while you are waiting, sit and listen to your child reading books – some from school, some from home – that they enjoy. As you share these books, you will spot the detail of their progress, their daily steps to independence. And even then, they will still love you reading to them.

There's never been quite the depth of appeal for adults in children's literature as there is today

CREATING STORIES

Why not create stories with your children? Ask them first about what characters they want in the story, where it is set, and any major event that should happen. You don't need a plot. You don't need an ending. You just need to start by inventing the first line. Then they tell you the next bit and it's back to you and so on. A story can be made up at bedtime, or in the day on a computer. You can print it out, illustrate it, and staple it into a book. Or just enjoy chatting about it for a few minutes.

Increased interest in books such as *Harry Potter* and *Lord Of The Rings* that are enjoyed by both adults and children is being reflected in a large rise in the number of parents reading to their children. A recent UK survey found that 90 per cent of parents read to their children at night compared with 40 per cent five years ago. A study of Finnish fathers who read frequently to their infants between 14 and 24 months of age found that, when these children grew older, they were much more interested in books than those children who had not been read to.

Puberty and sex education

You may have received little parental guidance as you went through puberty, relying, instead, on what you picked up in the playground. But a modern dad cannot afford to leave his sons and daughters so adrift.

The big change

One minute your kids are running around naked and everyone's cool about it. The next, they are suddenly more self-conscious as their bodies metamorphose in often awkward and confusing ways until eventually they achieve an adult equilibrium.

Girls and puberty

Sex hormones can begin the process of change in girls as early as 8, although puberty does not usually kick in until 11. The first signs are usually the development of breasts and then of pubic hair. Acne, greasiness of the skin and scalp, and body odour all follow. She will usually have a gawky, adolescent growth spurt, with her hands and feet growing disproportionately at first, followed by her legs and her spine. As fat redistributes itself to her breasts and hips, she begins to gain womanly curves. Your baby has definitely grown up. However, she will probably not have her first period until she is 12 or 13, though good nutrition means that periods are starting younger. It is vital that she understands what is coming so that her first period is not a sudden and terrible shock.

Boys and puberty

Boys hit puberty about six months after girls, typically around age 12 (though it can be younger) when the testicles enlarge, followed typically within six months by the development of pubic hair and growth of the penis. His adolescent growth spurt comes later, at about 14, as do the other signs of puberty: underarm hair, greasiness of the skin, acne, with the development of facial hair starting at about 15. But by then his voice will probably have broken, a process that begins at about 13. Just as girls need to understand periods before they happen, it is important that you explain to your son about "wet dreams" (nocturnal ejaculation), which are perfectly normal, but might upset him. This ejaculation shows he is producing semen, so, if you haven't got around to explaining the facts of life by now, you'd better start talking fast.

Sexual development

Girls and boys typically play well together until about 7 when they might seek out their own sex and sometimes become quite hostile to the opposite sex. This segregation usually begins to end at about 11, though there are no hard-and-fast rules. Remember, although kids talk about boyfriends and girlfriends from about 7, it is a mistake to put an adult interpretation on their language. It is also worth remembering that sexual activity of young people is generally over-estimated, both by over-anxious adults and bragging young people. About a third of girls and fewer boys have had sexual intercourse by 16.

Handle with care

It is very important to be sensitive to the changes a child goes through. As she gets older and more aware of her body, she might not want to have baths with younger siblings. She might, after years of being oblivious, be embarrassed to find you and your partner naked in bed together. Make sure her increasing need for privacy is respected.

AGONY UNCLE

Q: What do I say if my 8 year old suddenly asks me a really detailed question on sex? I want to be honest, but not tell her too much too early.

A: Don't panic. You can stall for time. Tell her it is a good question and you would like to give it a little thought. That gives you time to seek some advice if you need it, without putting your daughter off asking in the future. You can check out a book, perhaps even find one you can show her, coming back to her with answers when you are ready.

It is very important to be sensitive to the changes a child goes through

SEX EDUCATION: YOUR ROLE

You cannot rely on school to tell your child everything he needs to know about sex. Between 5 and 7, children learn about animal and human reproduction, with more detail at junior level. However, they need your help understanding how all this fits into relationships. Boys in particular need support as girls also have an informed magazine culture to guide them. The rule of thumb is to take your lead from your child. Wait until he asks a question. Answer honestly, but bear in mind that a five year old needs less detail than an 11 year old requires.

teenage *years*

So, you thought it was tough being a dad so far? Just wait. Suddenly your cute little daughter is **growing curves, dating boys**, and throwing more tantrums than a Hollywood diva. Meanwhile your son's turned into a big, hairy, smelly, growling lump who can **look you right in the eye**. And what about you? Where did that gut come from? Where did that hair go? **When did you become an old fart?** Welcome to the teenage years, pal. **They're going to be a wild ride**.

Being a **role model**

A teenager's dad is a bank manager, late-night taxi driver, phone provider, homework tutor, relationship counsellor, and crisis manager. But above all, he's an example.

Decision-makers

Teenage kids are caught halfway between childhood and adulthood. For the first time in their lives they are making vital decisions for themselves, trying to work out who they are, what they're going to become, and how they relate to the world around them.

The choices they make about education or possible careers will affect their entire lives. That sudden weight of responsibility can be overwhelming. So teens are caught between the longing for independence and the need for security. Don't be fooled by their apparent indifference; they still need you and your guidance.

Do as I say...

You're a vital role model in your child's life. So do you back up your words by being honest, fair, reliable, and loving? Or are you a hypocrite who says one thing and does another? Your kids will know the difference and it will hugely affect their respect for you.

Being there

"Your dad doesn't have to do anything special," says Holly, 17. "It's often just being there to talk to, or have a laugh, or give you a lift if you're late for school." But being there can be difficult. By the time your children reach their teens, there's a big chance you won't be living with them, due to divorce or a broken relationship. But you can remain a positive presence in their lives and it makes a big difference. Many researchers believe that teenagers without fathers in their lives are less likely to succeed at school and more likely to have drink, drug, sexual, or legal problems.

Getting back in touch

If you've been cut out of your children's lives, take heart. As teens become more independent, with their own phones and computers, they often restore contact you feared was lost. Even the moodiest teenager wants to love their parents; you owe it to them to deserve their love.

TERRY'S STORY

"My marriage broke up when my son Anthony was nine. I was only allowed to see him once a month. After I'd given him back, I'd just sit in the car, weeping.

"Things got worse. For three years, I couldn't even speak to him. Then, when he was 15, Anthony called to ask if he could come and live with me. It was wonderful being back together. We spent endless hours talking about girls, love, work, sport, life, you name it. When he left school, the yearbook described him as 'morally and intellectually the star of the year'. I felt such a sense of achievement.

"Anthony's in his twenties now. We're still very close. We see each other at least once a week. I hope I've helped him to become a man."

SONS

If you want to know what kind of man your son will become, take a good look in the mirror. He'll have learned his biggest lessons from you.

The way you treat the women in your life will have a huge influence on your son's own relationships. Your attitudes to schoolwork and careers will influence his own aspirations.

A father's love can be inspirational. As Grand Prix star Jenson Button recalls, "My dad used to take me karting. He'd borrow a car to get there. Then he'd borrow more money to run the kart and get home, because he was struggling so much financially. But he'd never stop me racing. He knew it was what I loved doing."

A father's failure can also be a spur. Some sons watch their abusive or absent fathers with contempt and swear that they will never be that kind of man themselves. And that, in the end, is the true test. Will your son be proud of the lessons his father taught him? Or will he be shamed by your example? It's really up to you.

DAUGHTERS

Women today are just as likely to have high-flying careers as men. So you owe it to your daughter to inspire her with the belief that she can succeed.

Of course, it's not the same having daughters as sons. There will be areas of her new life as a woman that a teenage girl will only want to share with her mother – thank goodness!

But there's one crucial way in which you are a daughter's role model: The first man a little girl ever loves is her father. The way that you respond to that love has a massive effect on her attitude to men in later life.

If her father loves her, gives her a sense of self-worth, and proves that men can be trustworthy, a teenage girl will have faith in the decency of men, the possibility of happiness, and her right to be treated with respect.

During her teens, your daughter will take her first steps into the world of adult relationships. It's never an easy road, but she'll stride out with a lot more confidence if she's secure in her father's love.

DAUGHTER TALK

Lorraine rose from a humble background to an successful media career. Asked how she did it, she replies "It starts with your parents. My father, in particular, never put a ceiling on my ambitions".

Mapping out:
the teenage years

When you're a teenager, you promise yourself you'll never be as uncool, as boring, as completely clueless as your dad. Then you become a dad and you have teens and you turn into that grumpy old man. Why? Because you've got teenagers to look after, of course.

They'll do...

10 things your children can or will do in their teens:

1 Discover sex (and hopefully love, too)

2 Get drunk

3 Experiment with drugs

4 Get into trouble

5 Learn to drive

6 Go to college

7 Earn money for themselves

8 Go on holiday without you

9 Live away from home

10 Know things you don't

...you'll say

10 things you thought you'd never say...but you will:

1 Turn that noise down!

2 You're not going out of the house dressed like that

3 You're grounded!

4 You need to take more exercise

5 You can't stay over with your friends unless you finish your homework first

6 Who was that boy/girl I saw you with?

7 Just because I did it, doesn't mean you have to

8 Stand up straight!

9 Music was much better when I was your age

10 No child of mine will...

Teenage **rebellion**

In *The Wild Ones*, the first great film about youth rebellion, someone asks Marlon Brando, "What're you rebelling against?" Brando sneers, "Whaddya got?". Even in the happiest families, most teenagers test the boundaries. They're establishing their independence, becoming their own people. Teen fashions, music, and attitudes have always been based on challenging oldsters and deriding their values. It can hurt sometimes to be on the receiving end, but there's not much you can do about it.

Make a difference

"Whaddya got?" is a deeper question than it seems. The environment you create can make the difference between harmless acting-up and serious trouble. A settled family and a good income don't guarantee well-adjusted children. Low-income, single-parent families are certainly not bound to fail. But the more deprived teenagers are in terms of education, housing, and emotional stability, the more likely they are to suffer problems ranging from criminal activity to underage pregnancy.

A father may not earn a fortune, but he can make a massive difference by being there to support his children and their mother. That's true in any social group, anywhere in the world.

Danger signs

So listen to your kids. Respect their opinions. Be honest about your own feelings: are you really acting in their interests? Above all, watch out for the danger signs. These include: disrupting school classes or truanting; hanging out with kids who misbehave; harming themselves or others; displaying over-sexualized behaviour; showing signs of depression or low self-esteem; and using drugs. The more of these symptoms your child displays, the more they need help. Make sure you are there to give it to them.

My kid, the criminal

The most serious form of rebellion is breaking the law. According to a recent Crime and Justice Survey:

- Young males aged 14–17 commit more crimes than any other group.
- One third of teenage boys have committed a "core" offence, such as theft, assault, drug-dealing, or criminal damage within the past 12 months. One-quarter have carried a weapon.
- Every year, one in eight teen girls commits a crime.
- Violent crimes by young women rose by 15 per cent in 2003–4.
- Most victims of teen crime are other teenagers (your kids are in more danger now than at any other time of their lives).

The facts are shocking. But they need a few words of caution:

- Most assaults do not cause serious injury.
- Most property crimes cause less than £100's worth of damage or loss.
- Just one crime in 100 ends up in a court appearance.

There's no need to panic. Most teenagers grow out of their misbehaviour. It is a small hard core of persistent offenders that accounts for 80 per cent of all crime.

DAD TALK

"My father sacrificed his life so that I could get a good education and he thought I was wasting it, going off to play rock music in this group called Queen. He hardly wanted to speak to me for a while.

"Then, much later, he saw us play Madison Square Garden in New York. He said, 'I'm so envious. You've achieved more in your life than I'm ever going to'. It was a terrible moment for me. I said, 'Dad, you're part of this'. "After that our relationship was much stronger. It wasn't long before he died, so it was important to straighten all that stuff out.

"I only realize now how much pain I caused my dad. It's the most painful thing when you experience that kind of rejection from a child, as I'm finding with my children now. I know it's inevitable, but boy, it kills you. When you're a kid you have no concept of how it would be impossible for a parent to want to hurt their child. I'd die for my kids."
Brian May, Queen guitarist

Talking about
sex and relationships

It's important to respect your children's privacy. They won't welcome you barging into their private lives. That said, teens like to pretend that they know it all. They absolutely do not. Make sure that they understand the risks involved in sex and the precautions that are required.

Teenage pregnancy

A double standard applies to the sex-lives of teenage boys and girls. Some dads are delighted when their son starts sleeping with girls – they don't feel that way when their daughter starts sleeping with guys. Of course, girls are the ones that get pregnant. But amidst the media hysteria about the slipping standards of girls today, it's important to put things in perspective. If, as one survey claimed, one girl in five has had sex by the time she's 14, four in five have not. If 46 girls in 1,000 give birth before the age of 18, 954 do not.

Feeling happy and secure

The average teenager loses his or her virginity at the age of 17. Kids who are promiscuous at an early age may have other problems in their lives. Sex can give them a sense of being valued that they do not get elsewhere. If your kids feel good about themselves, they are more likely to have sex because they want to, not because they're pressured into it. And that sex is more likely to be part of a genuine, loving relationship.

Boys are sensitive, too

It's worth remembering that the standard male-female stereotypes are often inaccurate. Boys may act as if sex is the only thing on their minds. A lot of the time it is. But they're more sensitive and emotionally vulnerable than they care to admit.

Homosexuality

Contrary to the standard belief that one person in 10 is homosexual, modern research suggests that there is roughly a three per cent chance of your child being gay or lesbian. That three per cent needs your love and support, too.

STAYING OVER

What do you do when your child wants to share a bedroom with her partner? Well, make sure they're both over 16. You're condoning a breach of the law if they're not.

- Talk the situation through with your child. It's his life, but it's your house. Together, come to an arrangement that suits everyone.

- Next, find out if the other parents are happy about the idea. They're counting on you to look after their child.

- Finally, think of the girl, whether she's your daughter or not. Does she need a room of her own, in case her decision is "no"?

- When kids have got a steady relationship, there's no reason to object. But if they're just starting out, why force the issue?

Drink and drugs:
telling them straight

Teenagers will be offered drugs and are likely to experiment, at least once. Chances are they'll get drunk, too. But it's one thing having a good night out. It's another becoming addicted. Danger-signs include listlessness and depression; a sudden decline in school grades or behaviour; stealing your money or valuables; pallid skin; bloodshot eyes; sudden changes in weight or appetite; and hanging out with new, undesirable friends. Teenagers are bombarded by media propaganda that makes binge-drinking and drug-taking seem cool. It's no fun being a party-pooper, but it's your job to tell them the risks.

DRUGS: THE HIGHS AND LOWS

Alcohol

High: Initial feelings of euphoria, confidence, sociability, and lowered inhibitions.

Damage: Excess consumption of alcohol leads to loss of co-ordination, slurred speech, slowed reactions, depression, aggression, and sexual impotence. Alcohol is addictive, with potentially fatal effects on the liver, kidneys, heart, and mental health. Alcohol damages the female reproductive system and harms unborn babies. At 100 calories per unit, alcohol can make you gain weight and will also ruin your skin (dryness, redness, blotchiness).

Cigarettes

High: Nicotine in tobacco aids relaxation and alertness.

Damage: Nicotine is rapidly addictive, with severe withdrawal symptoms. Tobacco smoke can cause cancer of the mouth, throat, and lungs and damages the heart. It is also harmful to pregnant women and their unborn babies. On average, smokers lose seven years from their lives and a fortune from their bank account. In the meantime, their breath smells, their skin wrinkles, and their teeth and fingernails turn brown.

Cannabis

High: Brings feelings of being relaxed and spaced-out, can be hallucinogenic in extra-strong "skunk" form.

Damage: Side-effects of smoke-inhalation are similar to cigarettes (*see above*), while cannabis itself is a factor in road-accidents, loss of academic and career motivation, and is believed to double the risk of severe mental illness, including schizophrenia. It also makes you dull company and causes you to crave junk food, which will lead to weight gain.

Ecstasy

High: Small doses make the user feel warm, affectionate, filled with energy, and able to dance for hours.

Damage: By affecting the brain's serotonin uptake, ecstasy may cause insomnia, depression, nausea, and blurred vision. It can also cause long-term memory-loss and mental health problems. Short-term dangers arise from impure drugs or extreme dehydration brought on by too much dancing in hot surroundings without sufficient fluid intake.

Cocaine

High: Initial feelings of euphoria, energy, self-confidence, and mental clarity.

Damage: Cocaine is addictive and can lead to paranoid psychosis, hallucinations, memory loss, abdominal pain, heart problems, and strokes. Combining coke and alcohol increases the risk of sudden death. "Crack" cocaine is even more addictive and dangerous than regular powder. Regularly snorting cocaine can also lead to a loss of sense of smell, nosebleeds, and problems with swallowing.

Heroin

High: Initial effects verge from blissful euphoria, through drowsiness and heavy limbs to nausea and shortness of breath.

Damage: Quickly addictive, heroin requires increased doses to have any effect. The withdrawal symptoms are severe and include muscle and bone pain, insomnia, vomiting, diarrhoea, and cold flashes with goose bumps. Injection of the drug leads to an increased risk of HIV and hepatitis. Other risks include fatal overdoses, an inability to function in day-to-day life, and resorting to crime to fund the habit.

Home life: cutting a deal

It's easy to treat the teenage years like one long series of
crises. But most of the time, you're all just trying to get
along the best you can. And that's not impossible. If you
love your kids and enjoy their company (most of the time!),
there's no reason why you can't have a good relationship.

Respect each other's rights

The key to this relationship is mutual understanding and respect. Both you and your teenagers need to know what is expected of one another:

You have the right to:

 Consideration. Adolescence is so overwhelming it can make teens self-obsessed. They must think about your needs too.

 Help. Your kids get free meals, transport…everything. So it's not too much to ask them to wash the dishes or take out the trash.

 Information. You don't want to snoop on your kids. But it makes it a whole lot easier to look after them if they let you know what's going on in their lives.

 Set boundaries. You don't have the right to be a dictator but you can establish basic moral standards in your own home.

 Take action. Sometimes you have to do things your children don't like because you genuinely feel it's for the best. It's tough. But that's your job as a parent.

Your children have the right to:

 Consideration. This cuts both ways. It's hard to believe sometimes, but teenagers are people, too.

 Privacy. Don't barge into their rooms without knocking and don't snoop in closets or computer-files without a serious reason to do so. Even then, think twice.

 Consultation. If a decision's going to affect them – from going on holiday to moving house – ask for their opinions first.

Trust. If you automatically assume that your children are deceiving you, or doing wrong, then you have got problems.

Childhood. You're the dad, they're the kids. They're supposed to dump their worries, crises, and broken hearts on you, not the other way round.

AGONY UNCLE

Q: My 15-year-old daughter goes out at night with her friends. If I ask her where she's going, she just says "Someone's house," or "Into town". If I ask her for an address, she says she doesn't know, or complains that I'm trying to interfere. Am I being unreasonable, wanting to know where she's going to be, or who she's going out with?

A: No. This comes under the headings of "consideration" and "information". Your daughter should accept, and even welcome, the fact that you care about her and worry about her, even if she doesn't think you need to. So it's not too much to ask a child, particularly one under 16, what her plans are. On the other hand, you should also trust her if she says there's nothing to worry about. If you seriously think she may be mixing with a bad crowd, or doing things she shouldn't, then you need to talk about it honestly and openly with her before things get out of hand. That comes under the heading of "take action".

Good food rules

As parents, we worry about our children taking drugs, abusing alcohol, or smoking. But arguably the biggest single threat to their health is what's in the fridge. Our kids eat too much and exercise too little. Obese teens risk the early onset of conditions such as diabetes and heart problems that were once the preserve of the middle-aged and elderly. They potentially face a lower life-expectancy than their parents.

Fat nation

Roughly 15 per cent of teenagers are now classified as obese or overweight (by contrast, less than one per cent risk anorexia nervosa, the potentially fatal self-starvation syndrome). Five out of six kids fail to eat the recommended weekly levels of fruit and vegetables. Meanwhile the average teenager spends £20 or more a month on sweets, crisps, processed snacks, and fizzy drinks.

Health time bomb

"Adolescents are the only age-group whose health is getting worse", according to Russell Viner, consultant in adolescent medicine at Great Ormond Street Hospital, London. Other experts have described youth obesity as a health time bomb. They point to a variety of causes for the problem. Traditional, home-cooked family meals have been replaced by much more informal, haphazard "grazing". Fresh ingredients have been replaced by junk food.

Do it together

The decline in sports at school has also made teenagers less fit. They're less likely to be walking, riding bikes, or playing football in the park; more likely to be watching television or playing video games. Health clubs that charge high prices or ban under-16s make it even harder for teens to take exercise.

But this is a problem you and your kids can solve together. Chances are, you're putting on a few pounds by now, yourself. So do everyone a favour: cut the junk, up the veggies, and get moving.

THE WORLD'S HEALTHIEST FOODS

According to a 2004 study by the Journal of Agricultural and Food Chemistry, the 14 foods listed below contain the most health-giving, age-defying vitamins, antioxidants, proteins, and fibres. The younger people start eating them, the more benefits they provide.

1. Blueberries
2. Red kidney beans
3. Pinto beans
4. Cranberries
5. Small Red beans
6. Artichoke hearts
7. Blackberries
8. Dried prunes
9. Raspberries
10. Strawberries
11. Red Delicious apples
12. Granny Smith apples
13. Pecan nuts
14. Sweet cherries

FOOD AND FITNESS

It's all about balance. The solution to obesity and being underweight are the same. Eat sensibly. Exercise regularly. Don't crash diet or overeat.

- **Eat breakfast** A healthy start to the day, providing energy and discouraging sugary snacks, is the basis of a well-balanced diet.

- **Start walking** The simplest way of taking exercise is just to walk to school and to the shops instead of going by car.

- **Make exercise fun** Exercise doesn't have to mean conventional sport. It can be dancing, roller-blading, or mountain-biking, too.

- **Family meals** Eat and cook family meals together regularly (*see panel right*) to ensure your children don't fill up on junk.

COOK TOGETHER

A healthy diet requires the right balance of carbohydrates, fats, and protein. To encourage your teenagers to eat right, start cooking with them, choosing healthy, staple foods, and teaching them the basics:
- cooking pasta
- creating sauces
- making stir-frys
- grilling meat and fish
- baking potatoes
- preparing salads
- boiling eggs
- making fruit smoothies

School gets serious

How successful do you want your children to be? The evidence is overwhelming: The better your kids' education, the greater their chances of finding a decent job, earning good money, and living a longer, healthier life. During their teens, your children will confront a far greater burden of schoolwork than ever before. Many of their exam marks will depend partly upon coursework, completed at home in their own time. And those marks will have a big influence on their ability to move on to higher education.

THE RACE FOR UNIVERSITY

British children have an extremely heavy exam burden, with major national exams in each of their last three years at school.

GCSEs

- Your kids will need at least five GCSE passes, grade A–C, to progress to further education. English and Maths are vital.

- Top universities, whose degrees are most valued by employers, can require several A-grade GCSEs to guarantee an interview.

A-Levels

- A-Levels are now taken in two instalments. Typically students sit four A/S Levels in Year 12, then three A/S Levels in Year 13.

- Some university courses may demand particular subjects at A-Level. But your kids will retain their motivation best if doing the subjects they enjoy the most.

Aiming high

The huge expansion in university education means that many children now have aspirations and expectations that are new to their parents. Your children may be aiming higher than you ever did, learning things you never knew. The education they receive now, as teenagers, is vital in enabling them to achieve these aspirations.

Too cool for school

Teenage boys statistically perform less well at school than girls. Your daughter is much more likely to get good exam results than your son, because girls tend to be more mature than boys in their teens. They are, on average, more willing to take time and care over coursework. But a big problem is a bias against learning among male pupils themselves. Many boys feel that academic success is "girly". They would rather be cool than work hard. For your son's sake, tell him: "real men pass exams".

Take action

The single best thing you can do for your teenager is not to let him get away with bunking off school or failing to hand in homework. Step in and take action if you think your child is falling behind. You have the right to get involved in his education and ensure that he is given the best possible head-start for the future.

Be supportive

Coursework and exams can be more emotionally draining on your children, and on yourself, than you might imagine. Make sure that you are there to support them – to give them the encouragement and confidence that they'll need to achieve good results.

Zen-like calm

It's important to provide a stable environment and a constant routine, and to be a calming influence. Children can get worked up and stressed over coursework problems and you need to be calm and encouraging to help keep them focused. This may be a challenge after a long day at work – but it is vital.

Make sure you're supportive and give them the encouragement and confidence they need

Access to information

Stock your home with reference books and make sure that your children have access to public libraries. If you can, try to provide a computer with Internet access – a great learning resource. Many public libraries also provide this service for free.

The value of **money**

Bob has two teenage sons. He loves them, so naturally he likes to provide for them. "My dad always messed me around with money," Bob says. "So I always make sure my boys have got enough. I don't want them to be flash, but I don't want them to feel poor, either. Whenever they go out, I'm happy to give them £20. There's a difference between indulging your kids and spoiling them." Many people would praise Bob for his generosity. Others would feel he's over-indulgent. They'd say teenage children need to learn the value of money and get used to the idea of fending for themselves, not waiting for handouts from dad. There's a balance to be struck.

If your kids have worked or saved hard to buy something, they'll appreciate it far more

An expensive business

Whatever your views, money is a major issue. Money worries trouble 35 per cent of teens. Meanwhile 23 per cent of parents are concerned by their teen's over-spending. It's not surprising. Being a teenager is an expensive business. Teenage kids want new clothes, CDs, DVDs, MP3 players, and mobile phones. They want concert tickets, meals and drinks, and travel expenses. And many need cash for gap years and college fees, too.

Where it all goes

Parents, meanwhile, are faced with offspring who travel full-fare on holidays and go on expensive school trips abroad. They agonize over their children's prospective college debts – up to £20,000 for many graduates – and wonder if they can help. And then, if their children are lucky, there's that first car and those massive insurance bills.

Be honest and fair

Different families will reach different conclusions, depending on their own financial circumstances. But try to be honest: if your children understand what you can and cannot afford, they'll know what they can reasonably expect. Most dads want to provide for their children – that's natural. But money isn't everything. Don't worry if you can't afford to splash out – your time and involvement mean a lot more to your kids than cash.

TEENS AND THEIR CASH FLOW

1 Make it clear what you will provide – say, school-related expenses – and what they must buy for themselves: CDs, make-up, computer-games, trips out with friends.

2 Pay a regular monthly allowance, and don't give in to whining if they spend it all too soon.

3 Set up bank accounts to encourage financial responsibility.

4 Encourage a part-time or Saturday job, so long as it doesn't interfere with school work.

5 Reward your kids by matching any money they can save or earn to pay for specific projects, such as gap-year travel or a school trip.

6 Don't be a Scrooge. The occasional unexpected gift makes everybody happy.

Letting **go**

Yes, they can be a pain sometimes. And the teenage years are tricky. But they're still your kids. You love them. You like having them around. And then, one day, they're off .